SINGING MY WAY AROUND THE WORLD

(An Entertainer's Life At Sea)

BY MIKE GOMBORONE

Illustrations by Mike Gomborone

CHAPTER TITLES

Chapter 1:

PREFACE

So how did I end up singing and dancing on cruise ships for three years?

Easy.

I needed the work. I had done summer stock, national tours, and performed in regional theaters. It was time to see the rest of the world.

At first, ships were just another way for me to keep active as a performer, but then the travel bug bit hard and took up permanent residence within me. It usually took about six months back ashore for me to realize how much I missed the seafaring life including visiting exotic ports, meeting many different people, and living rent-free!

I used to accept contracts based on what new parts of the world I'd visit. On Holland America's Rotterdam, Alaska, Hawaii, and some of the South Pacific were covered. On the Royal Viking Sun, I circumnavigated South America and saw Asia and Australia. Then with the Cunard Caronia, I sailed into the Mediterranean and Baltic for the first time. On subsequent trips, Guatemala and the Amazon were explored. With later ship contracts, I didn't concern myself with the itinerary anymore. I just wanted to be back afloat.

My camera had fresh batteries, the sunscreen was slathered on, and I was in full tourist mode, map and all. There was always something new to see no matter where I ended up.

Anchors aweigh!

Chapter 2:

INTRODUCTION

This ship is an absolute mess.

My cast has arrived at our home for the next six months: the Cunard Caronia. However, the vessel sits uselessly on museum-like display within the confusing confines of the Bremerhaven, Germany shipyard. "Dry-docked" for refurbishment and repairs, its hull is completely out of the water, magically balancing on a few blocks within a massive sunken pit.

We drag our numerous bags (six months worth of stuff!) over a steep, rickety, and oh yes, wet gangway. It's been pouring since we landed.

Having just flown in from the States, jet lag heavily dulls us. A fine powder (probably sawdust) coats the reception area as we enter, the carpets half pulled up, and the golden couches covered in durable opaque plastic. Have we made a terrible mistake?

Through some mix-up in the main office, we were not expected until two days later. All of our rooms lie in gritty disarray; none of them have running water. Nobody knows where to put us and only four passenger rooms operate with working showers. We must sign up for a time slot, bringing all of our toiletries and towels up with us from several decks down. This information is not sitting well. I suppose we could just grab some soap and get naked outside since the melancholy sky still pours. Our female vocalist is slowly breaking down before our eyes.

A couple of cast members worked on the ship before, so they lead us down behind the "crew only" doors and into the metallic guts to locate the office of the crew purser where each one of us has to sign a pile of paperwork. We are led down into what seems like miles of winding halls and through dangerous-looking watertight doorframes, heavy and thick, guarded by bright red alarm bells.

We dodge the many welders and deck staff dressed in oily blue coveralls and while everyone is friendly, I am completely lost. I will never learn my way around this maze. I'm like Kate Winslet during "Titanic", in that long hallway with no clue of what direction to go and an ocean of water hurling at me. Frustration sets in as I remember that this is the smallest ship I have ever worked on!

We climb down more stairs, round a couple corners, and the pot of gold at the end of our tarnished rainbow appears, the crew purser's office. There's no way that I will ever find this place again on my own. Our signatures dutifully entered into the ship's log, we become "official". We surrender our passports and have our photos snapped for identification cards. Perfect timing. We couldn't look more haggard, jetlagged, wet, lost, dirty, and frustrated, yet these pictures will "identify" us for the next six months.

The crew bar is a cozy space where all of the crew can hang out and just be themselves. No uniforms have to be worn, nobody has to unwillingly smile, and the drinks are very inexpensive. All of the lights are on, revealing a well worn, ugly blue linoleum floor, and the television blares CNN as a couple stewards on their break play cards while others compete at the pool table. Through the stale smoke that hovers in the air, they look up and smile at our weary faces.

As production cast members, my eight co-workers and I have the best of two worlds: that of passenger or crew. Since our other two guys are coupled with their girlfriends, I luck out and get a single cabin. Most other crewmembers are four to a room and share a communal bathroom.

Our mini orientation continues in the ballroom where we have an impromptu meeting with our cruise director and his assistant. They run the entertainment department and brief us on our responsibilities, in terms of uniform, decorum, and our limited duties outside of the shows.

The ballroom floor, where we had intended to rehearse and set our shows in their proper space, is covered with stacked chairs. This sad and dark space could never be elegant.

The current state of this room and our increasing struggle to stay alert prompts our company manager to conclude that we must adjourn until tomorrow. Our producer has granted clearance for us to book hotel rooms in town for the night. We need some quiet, we need clean air, and we need to adjust to our new time zone.

Much more refreshed, we arrive back at the Caronia the next day. It is remarkable to see how quickly the ship is put back together especially when passengers are due on in seven days! Most are repeat customers and once the vacuuming stops, the plastic clears, and the glass sparkles once again, it is easy to see why.

As long as we follow the evening's dress code, we can use any space on the ship (except bar stools and the casino) and socialize with passengers. During the day, we can attend any movies and lectures that we want to, as well. The main rule is to remember that the passengers (paying customers) come first. If there are no seats left for a passenger during a lecture, you do not stay and listen yourself. If there are passengers behind you at the buffet line, you let them go ahead. Rules can be bent for us in terms of eating in the dining room if family members are onboard for a cruise, but special permission must be granted from the cruise director, dining room manager, and hotel manager, the ship's social bigwigs.

Most other crewmembers are not allowed these perks, sequestered strictly to crew areas. These also include the crew pool and sunbathing deck that are at the front (the rockiest part) of the ship.

We also benefit from the social life of the crew. Guest entertainers (those onboard to perform specialty shows), for example, are not allowed in the crew areas for insurance purposes. We are, though, being fully trained crewmembers.

Yes, the ship is small, but even within the first week onboard, I feel like we know a majority of the crew. After five weeks rehearsing in an airless Florida studio, we're ready for our new luxurious lifestyle.

Following much more shipboard rehearsal, and finally settled into my cabin, I study the itinerary. I'm getting PAID to travel to twenty-five countries in six months! Most of my working hours are in the evening, so days are free to explore the ports.

The Shore Excursion office always needs one escort per tour bus in each port. The escort counts passengers to make sure that nobody is left behind, fills out the report on how everything was operated, and enjoys all aspects of the tour free of charge. Perhaps I can get in on that, yet another perk to my already amazing job.

In Dover, England, passengers embark. For the first of many times, we man our lifeboat drill stations. I partner with the chief photographer. He checks off everyone's names as they report in and I ensure that all the neon orange lifejackets are worn properly…

"Yes, ma'am, you must put it on. I'm sorry it doesn't match your gold lame top."

"No, sir, your strap does NOT go through that loop in back. It must be kept free in case you must be retrieved from the ocean with a hook."

I chuckle to myself, observing how many interesting variations there are in lifejacket donning:

"Um, sir? Your jacket's on upside down!"

By international maritime law, these drills occur within the first twenty-four hours of every cruise for newly embarked passengers.

As all the newcomers slowly disperse, rolling up the straps of their jackets and strolling to the back deck for their free champagne sail away, I linger and enjoy the sun glinting on the water. The Baltic Sea is our destination, where we will do two or three cruises. Then we veer south and east to enter the Mediterranean Sea. Once we pass the Rock of Gibraltar, we have entered the playground that is to be ours for the rest of the summer.

Thus began my total of two years onboard the Cunard Caronia. My first shipboard job as a singer/dancer was on the old ss Rotterdam with Holland America and then I performed for another six months on the Royal Viking Sun.

If exempt from the tortures of seasickness, cruise ships are an ideal means for any adventurous traveler. Go to sleep off the coast of France and wake up in Italy without the hassle of airports and inconvenience of jet lag. These are some of my adventures and observations from three years worth of singing my way around the world.

Chapter 3:

THE WAR IS OVER

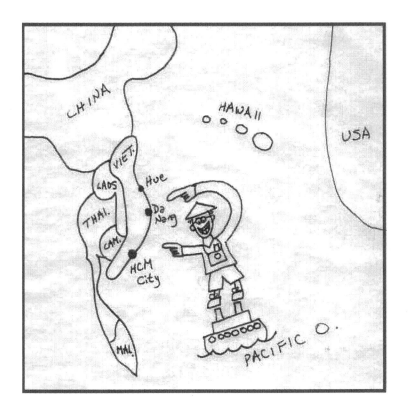

My alarm clock shocks me out of my warm sleep and I'm reluctant to expose myself to the air-conditioning of my cabin. Our last days of the Asia cruise drawing near, all of this travel is finally catching up to me. With only one or two days to explore each port, it's go, go, go or miss out!

Another escort form for a tour I've been assigned to has been slid under my door—a total of four in the next two days. Fantastic! I will see so much. But now I have to gather up and count the members of tour du jour number one, and meet Vietnam.

Vietnam. This is my first visit to a Communist country.

Communism!

Long forgotten feelings of fear well up inside of me here in Vietnam. Although Communism has left Russia, I was raised during the time when Russia (i.e. Communism) was "the enemy". They were going to nuke us back to the Stone Age at any given moment from what I was led to believe as a kid.

Communism still exists here in Vietnam. Plus, I have to come halfway across the earth to experience my first curfew ever, including four years of high school. Nobody is allowed to be outside of the dock area from 11 PM to 7 AM.

When I was growing up, Vietnam seemed a dismal and ruined war zone. Would I still see signs of destruction after so many years? Socializing the other day with a too well-traveled passenger (if that is possible), my trepidations regarding the country came into the conversation. She looked up at me, apparently having forgotten our itinerary, and grumbled, "Ugh, Vietnam again?"

"Vietnam AGAIN?!"

Was she serious? What was she talking about? Is the country in that bad of shape? Is it possible to be THAT jaded? Would it be safe for me, an American, to walk about on my own? All I know is what I've seen in movies or lectures. The anticipation of the four tours I'll be escorting have built my curiosity about Vietnam, but now I am not so sure how comfortable I'll be…

The passengers and I disembark and head for our tour bus. We are in a dockyard, so there is not much to be ascertained yet about the country, except for what can be judged by looking at the vendors' items: colorful outfits, charcoal drawings, small marble statuary, and always, jewelry.

Ho Chi Minh City, the former Saigon, is our goal. Up to now, the only

reference points I have for here are from the musical, "Miss Saigon".
Our guide is a very happy, enthusiastic, and helpful man. He wants us
to know everything about his country and city. Thousands of natives
plow through the narrow streets and we whiz by the Chinatown district.
Every large city we have visited thus far has had a Chinatown, so I find
myself wondering what's to be expected in China?

"Hey, let's go to...town!"...

Crawling with bicycles, rickshaws, and motorbikes, the traffic
somehow flows. Some people are wearing surgical masks as they ride
about. Others wear those pointy straw hats, so practical in the
unforgiving sun. The American Embassy looms ahead, the climax of
the Vietnam War, of "Miss Saigon".

All is calm now.

But back on the tour bus an hour later, claustrophobia has gripped the
passengers. Horrific traffic and oppressive heat are creating monsters.
Finally back from our simple city tour, a sudden sense of freedom fills
me as I meet some friends and we set off on our own. I don't have to
answer to anybody anymore today.

Rickshaws eagerly approach our party, two of us climbing into each
one, and we're pedaled off on a thrill ride through lane-less streets and
around scary curves, the danger of capsizing always imminent. Our
guide coaxes us into the very dense and dark Ben Thanh Market area.
Old, khaki tarps separate each vendor, religiously guarding their dingy,
used merchandise.

Eerie piles of American army uniforms, canteens, dog tags, and old
photographs FOR SALE meet our disbelieving eyes! Do tourists
actually buy these incredibly morbid items? For a while, I had forgotten
what had occurred here within my lifetime. Watches, lighters, and
chilling Viet Cong flags sit on display at the next station. As a kid, I
heard about a friend of the family who fought in this war and still

suffered mentally. How would he feel about all of this? I am more than happy to leave this market of horrors.

Everything is beginning to close and the sun is gone. Being out in this area too late is not our idea of fun. Traffic now madder than ever, our two rickshaws have become separated. For a fleeting moment, I imagine a kidnapping scenario. Our driver speaks not a word of English, and we not a word of Vietnamese. "Oh, relax", I tell myself, "You've seen too many movies." Making a safe return to our port, I am relieved to see that our friends have arrived, too.

The Cu Chi Tunnels, a preserved area where soldiers' barracks contain various displays demonstrating jungle warfare life, are our destination for the next day. My journal reads as follows:

What an experience. Just the maps and cross-sections alone were a clue to how big and awesome this "project" was. There was a video showing happy Vietnamese women weaving and cutting death spikes FOR US with pretty upbeat music playing in the background. We trekked out into the jungle and found the tiny hole covered in leaves that was the entrance to go down into the tunnel. I went first and hated it, but at least I was able to go through quickly. The walls were nothing but dirt. Imagine being down in there for hours at a time! We were shown the "hospital": a couple cots on a dirt floor set in a rickety structure with open windows. I would have rather died.

They kept a bomb crater intact, showing us how the weaponry was capable of destroying the first and second layers of the tunnels. God, to be trapped underground in a cave-in! The booby traps littered around were very effective in maiming. Someone would step on a flat surface that flipped over, exposing the ferocious spikes underneath, stabbing the leg in a multiple amount of locations. All of this was awful, but I couldn't help being fascinated.

Air holes were pointed out to us. The smoke holes from the kitchen had to be very far distant so that the main location of the fighters would not be given away. We were served taro and tea in the "meeting room", a basic shack. It was pretty good, but I can't imagine living on the stuff.

In the gift shop we met two New Zealand girls who were backpacking across the country. Would I be able to do that? I am spoiled by the amenities of ship life, knowing that I can escape back if I find a port unfavorable. Later we see a man making model helicopters out of soda cans—very clever. We had the chance to buy scorpion, snake, or seahorse wine, but none of us partook.

Later as we sail down the river, rural life unfolds: the huge fishing nets set out and checked by single men in their tiny long boats, homes on stilts looking as if they'll topple over at any moment, and palm trees, reminding us that we are in the tropics. Jarringly, a satellite dish pops up every so often, too.

Danang lies next on our itinerary. My tour today is to the ancient city of Hue (pronounced HWAY). The journey is very long, but Vietnam distracts us from our watches. Everything is green. I forgot how many shades of green are possible! Seductive mountains appear out of the haze. China Beach looks exactly as it did on the television show I vaguely remember. Incense bouquets are the prime focus of one town we pass through, selling buckets and buckets of them. Children, some still in diapers, run out of their family huts and greet us everywhere we go, always smiling. I would have run out of film if I took all of the pictures that I wanted to of their smiling golden faces.

The scope of the former city is staggering and the story of its downfall sad. Between French and American conflicts, most of the area was obliterated, the rubble cleared in 1980. All that remains are two elaborately recreated buildings (the gateway and the Thai Hua Palace), a few foundations, and stone steps that lead up to nowhere. My imagination has to fill in the rest. I am told that visiting the Forbidden City in Beijing, China is the closest experience of what Hue once was. Unfortunately, time does not permit for exploring the extensive, grassy grounds.

We lunch. A detailed pineapple dragon with garlic clove teeth greets us ferociously at the large buffet table. Little woven grass boxes containing sweet rice intrigue me the most. I dive into familiar spring rolls and enjoy dragon fruit, pink and spiky buds from cacti that contain white flesh with black seeds. They taste like a crunchy kiwi fruit.

That afternoon, at the exquisite grounds of the Tu Duc Tombs, full of mossy bridges and impossibly gnarled trees, part of a wall has just collapsed. It seems perfectly right to observe this ancient architecture rotting away.

All of these new sights in Vietnam have tired me, but our tour ends with a muted sunset behind a craggy mountain. Silhouetted round boats, featured in our foreground, contain fishermen wearing their ubiquitous conical hats.

A local show with exotic instruments, song, and dance is performed onboard. One piece features the skillful playing of a stone xylophone! However, another morphs into Western techno music. That I could have stayed in my cabin for. The buzz on the ship is that the overland tour to Laos missed its return flight, "stranding" them until the next available one!

I have one more day in Vietnam now, escorting a tour into the surrounding countryside of DaNang. Our guide is a beautiful young woman named Huong, which means "perfume". She impresses all of us by learning every single person's name on the bus. Huong later teaches us that the word "ma", depending upon which of five different tones it's pronounced with, means "mother" (in the north or center of the country), "tomb", "hawk", or "ghost"!

Strangely, both buses on this tour have gotten lost. We make a stop at a local fair, but nearby field workers with their water buffalos become our main focus. Climbing out of my bus, a woman has bashed onto the ground and cut her shin quite badly. We are in the middle of nowhere! Thank goodness the ship's nurse is the other bus' escort and with her first aid kit, she fixes up our lady quite nicely. The required accident report is completed and both Huong and I feel relieved that the woman has taken all of this in stride. I think she's more embarrassed than anything else.

At the end of our tour, having visited Marble Mountain and enjoyed the high pitched hammering music echoing from the numerous carving studios, Huong wishes us all one hundred years of happiness (!) and thanks me profusely for "all of my help". She was very upset by the injured woman and tells me, "I am having difficulty finding words to express how grateful I am to you"! Her sincerity touches me. I had done nothing more than alert the nurse. We hug each other good-bye.

I have developed a bit of a crush on my guide!

Last minute deals await us from the vendors near the ship. A charcoal print of a field worker with his handy buffalo and straw hat becomes my latest room decor. I carefully roll up my new treasure for safekeeping, appreciating how all of Vietnamese art features water, due to its importance to these wonderful people. I am, after all, a Pisces.

I'm grateful as the cool air of my cabin hits my skin. Naptime is next on my itinerary. Vietnam has surprised me. I had no idea that I'd enjoy educating myself on its culture and history so much and still can't believe the proximity of the war. Vietnam welcomed me, but sadly, I know that this is not the case for all Americans. But that was in the past. I am grateful to have experienced no prejudice or hostility due to my nationality.

"Vietnam again?"

I'd go back in an instant.

Chapter 4:

RESCUE AT SEA

4:30 AM.

Perhaps I shouldn't have stayed out so late.

Perhaps I shouldn't have moved to the party in our cruise director's cabin.

But it was our hump day, the exact middle of six months onboard the ol' ss Rotterdam. I can sleep in tomorrow...

5:40 AM.

I'm in bed and over the speaker, the captain announces that nearby there's a ship on fire and we're rescuing its passengers! How awful to be on a flaming vessel at sea. There is nowhere to escape but in the soup. During our initial onboard orientation, we are trained to have TWO escape routes from our cabins and work areas. With all of these small hallways within the ship, one could easily be blocked by smoke and/or fire.

Appearing eerily through the morning fog sits a smallish white ship with smoke belching out of its stern. The fire doesn't appear to be huge, but there's enough smoke to cause alarm. Four of our tenders are making multiple trips to the wounded vessel and bringing everyone over to our safe haven. How can our ship accommodate so many extra people? We are already on a sold out cruise!

How surreal is this? Picture frightened passengers bobbing around in three tenders waiting their turn as the first batch of all these folks gingerly unloads into the yawning entry of our ship. A question pops up as this panorama unfolds, "What would I take if I could bring only three things with me?" My priority would be my laptop computer, definitely.

Well, on second thought, never mind. Everyone must abandon all of their personal items AND their privacy. In an emergency, the only things allowed into lifeboats besides you are personal medications and warm blankets. Luxury goes down with the vessel.

Thank God WE'RE not on fire. All of those crewmembers must be losing their jobs. I'd be out thousands of dollars with half the summer left. I feel badly for them since most have to support a family somewhere…

…The latest news is that we're skipping Valdez, Alaska and going straight to Seward for an overnight in order to drop everyone off! All of these extra people are wandering around our ship like lost souls. They truly have NOWHERE to go. The pile of used lifejackets on deck is a formidable reminder of what's happened. The rescuees are wearing little orange dot stickers on their chests to signify that they can have free drinks! At least that's some consolation. Their cruise had just begun.

The weather is pretty nippy, yet no empty deck chairs can be found outside. People are lounging around our fancy ballroom and sitting areas as if at summer camp! I can't handle this chaos anymore. I hide in my cabin…

We're on CNN! I am on the Rotterdam watching footage of us rescuing everyone! US Coast Guard boats and helicopters are on the scene, too. I'll have to call my Mom and see if she finds an article about us in the paper!

One evening, a few years later, I'm hanging out in New York City with a friend and his roommate. We have been talking about our ship jobs and all of the crazy things that can happen at sea. Upon mentioning the fiery rescue, my friend's roommate excitedly screams about how she had been performing on that unfortunate ship, the Regent Star! I pull out my photo album with the pictures and we go over the articles recounting the incident. And yes, she did get sent home after the fire. It took several months to make the Star seaworthy again.

What a small world we live in!

Chapter 5

THE OTHER GREAT WALL

The Great Wall of China remains on my "To Visit" List. Until then, another wall shall serve as my personal favorite, the one surrounding Dubrovnik, Croatia.

Located on the east coast of the Adriatic (we would always be on our way to Venice), Dubrovnik had just reopened after the horrible ten-year war that ravaged its terra cotta roofed beauty. A map at the main gate into the city heartbreakingly plots all of the war damage from the bombing, but also demonstrates impressive proof of how much work went into restoring Dubrovnik back to the magical gem that it is.

The clean wall surrounding the city alone is enough reason to make the journey. I pay the minimal fee in the local currency, kunas, haul myself up some treacherous stairs along a powerful turret of stone, and just walk. Every step and corner is a photo opportunity, a bird's eye view of the ramrod straight streets and hypnotizing patterns of half-cylinder roof tiles. These panoramas are all mine! A woman rests her elbows on her windowsill, eating. Life is written all over her weary face. She has seen it all.

A tiny section of the city has not yet been refurbished. The weedy floors of the structures show through their rotting and gray roof tiles, serving as a sobering reminder of what the entire city must have looked like after the last onslaughts.

Somebody vacuums in their home. The sound is surprisingly anachronistic.

I descend from the great wall and hit the smooth stones on the main thoroughfare. They must be very slippery on rainy days. Cobbled side streets transform into remarkably steep hills for such a confined area within this wall. My thighs pulse as I scale another formidable stone staircase. I have no destination; I am in full exploration mode.

Laundry hangs out everywhere in the Mediterranean with Dubrovnik as no exception. Busy homes and playful children occupy these canyons. I am suddenly alone, but I can't get lost here. The wall ultimately keeps me safe.

Later, my friends and I savor a sunset from the wall. Hundreds of high-pitched and frenetic swallows fly outlined against the dusky sky. Our stomachs growl out that it's time to adventure forth for food.

English is pretty prevalent here, but only in the touristy central part of the city. We are the intrepid, though, who track off the beaten path and sponsor the motto: the less English spoken, the better.

Dark alleyways stretch up and lead into the labyrinth of family filled homes with various cooking smells emanating from them. The occasional cat crosses our path. Lee, from the Shore Excursion department, has a restaurant in mind that he has scoped out from the wall! We wander in that general direction as best we are allowed.

Another dead end is responsible for our cause to start losing its allure. Hunger! The dreaded direction asking is upon us. Most of the folks in the area don't speak English and a few simple hand gestures won't do, with all of these confusing byways to contend with.

We find a man and pose our question, but before we know it, we are IN his house! What's going on here? Is he going to cook for us? Talk about hospitality!

Wrong!

He's trying to sell us his current batch of homemade beverage: tangled weeds and mangled herbs suspended inside a used two-liter plastic bottle of green tea-colored liquid.

Hm.

My instinct is to politely decline and encourage everyone to be on our way. Lee, however, gives the man one US dollar for this concoction (!) and bravely twists off the cap to down some of the juice right in front of the enterprising Croatian.

Oh, Lee's face.

Priceless.

He has a pretty high tolerance for liquor, but this brew jolts. We can practically see the stuff rotting Lee's innards. Did the locals actually drink it? Was daily life is this charming city that harsh? Waving us away, the man's wife is delighted that we have done business with her bold husband.

Our restaurant has finally been found and we take turns initiating ourselves into Lee's select club. UGH! I can STILL taste it years later! A Draino chaser could have capped off this experience and I probably wouldn't have killed as many cells in the lining of my esophagus.

The home-brew we were suckered into buying became ship legend. In the end, nearly everyone of the crew had had at least a baby sip. The smell alone could cure the common cold. The hootch was eventually abandoned in the crew bar, free alcohol that even the biggest drinker onboard could not consume. THAT'S how bad it was.

At the end of my contract, I bottled a bit of the liquid up and sent it to Lee as a silly Christmas present, assuring the US Post Office that my little gag was properly sealed. That remaining had long since disappeared from the Caronia's crew bar. Perhaps it was unceremoniously dumped, having taken up too much precious space where much better quality liquor was available. Perhaps it was used to sanitize a toilet. I hope, though, that somewhere deep in the state of Washington, a little bit of this unforgettable elixir still exists, commemorating my first trip within the great wall of Dubrovnik.

Chapter 6:

A MOST EXOTIC BIRTHDAY

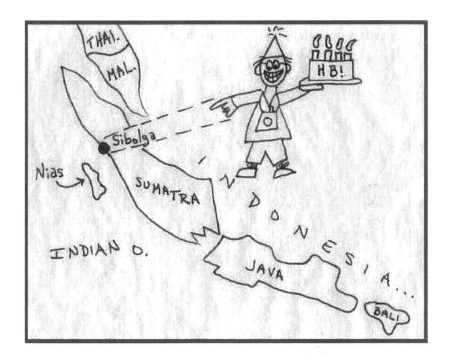

March 11 dawned and I found my ship anchored off of Sibolga, Sumatra, a small fishing village. It was my birthday and three cast friends and I hired a driver to take us around for a tour and teach us some local history.

Our way up to view the town from a looming mountain was treacherous. Our guide informed us that people died all the time when their buses ran off the road and into the steep gorge that ironically provided our wonderful scenery.

Anchored with a few tinier islands nearby, our ship looked very out-of-place amongst the alien fishing stations so common here. The locals built huts above the water that appeared to hover over enormous nets spread out for fishing. Looking spider-like, waiting for prey above their webs, the huts were scattered helter-skelter all along the coast.

Traversing our road at night was impossible. Besides the inherent danger of its curviness, tigers roamed about! By day, we had no luck seeing one of the fiery giants emerge from the jungle greenery. Our guide told us the grim truth that while the Sumatran tiger is very endangered, the Balinese and Java tigers have become extinct.

Our short tour over, we roamed through town on our own. At a very colorful and loud local market, a man gave me some sugar and cinnamon bark to chew on. I was reluctant to accept his gifts, distrustful of strangers giving things to me, but did not want to offend him and instinctively, I knew he was much more open and friendly than what I was used to back home.

Tangerines and a local fruit called salak became gifts for some children in exchange for their pictures. The woman who I bought the fruit from had settled on a blanket with her scale and goods piled around her. She let me take her photo. Although none of her few teeth showed, she displayed a very welcoming grin. Other unrecognizable fruits sat nearby in large woven baskets.

From this market we stumbled into the unmistakable drying racks for the fish. The malodorous air assaulting us did nothing to improve my life-long aversion to seafood. However, I found the local preservation techniques fascinating with their rustic simplicity.

Thick, flat pieces of wood resting on rack frames constructed out of thin poles supported loads of fish. None of this looked nailed together. These racks sat right at the water's edge so that the fish could be directly placed on them once ashore. Was salt even used, or just the sun? We couldn't tell. How long did the fish stay out like this to dry? We didn't know that either, but our noses and weak stomachs signaled the time to move along.

My Sibolga highlight was in meeting a group of eager school kids just finishing up their studies for the day. One boldly approached me to practice her English, her friends getting such a kick that I would take the time to talk to her. It was wonderful to connect with more locals and I was only too happy to indulge and let her ask me questions: what was my name, where was I from, and what was I doing there? I ended up telling her that it was my birthday and she let me take her picture, too. She spoke with such a strong accent, I thought she was telling me her name was "Fe-ro-NI-ka". How pretty! But then I saw her write down, "Veronica" and had to laugh--not as exotic as I had thought! Veronica also wrote down her address and I promised I'd write to her and send her a copy of our picture.

My friends and I hired a rickshaw to get us back to the ship and as we passed Veronica and her troop, she blew me a birthday kiss, completely melting my heart! I did write to her later, but never heard back. Had I misread her writing and sent the letter to some nonexistent address? Was it too expensive for her to write back to me?

In December of 2004, the horrible tsunami struck, effecting much of Indonesia. How did Sibolga, Sumatra fare? Did the fishermen lose all of their rickety racks and dried fish? How many perished? How is my smiling fruit vendor? Is she still in her spot that she seemed to have been in for her whole life selling fresh wares? The tigers are probably fine with their strange sixth sense that we humans are nowhere near to understanding.

But what about Veronica? Did she graduate from school? I hope that she's OK.

Chapter 7:

NEARLY NUDE, PART I

Guys were always lacking for the fashion show held by the shops onboard during each cruise. And because I entertain, it was assumed that I'd just love to hop right in and wear clothes designed for much older and bigger men. Others in my cast became involved, so the passengers got to know us faster.

We put on our clothes, entered the stage with our partners, and I would suddenly remember why I did NOT like being a fashion model.

Where was the choreography? Where was my microphone? What character was I playing?

…Me? I had to play just ME!?

That is not fun. If I wanted to play me, I could go up on deck and read my book. I could grab a teatime scone and WATCH the fashion show. But, no. I was in front of hundreds of people wearing hideous plaid shorts hanging down at my knees trying really hard to feel sporty.

Now one day I got to wear a very expensive emerald and diamond ring. That was fun. I was a king that afternoon. Another time, given cardboard guns and gussied up in tuxedos, we made spy-like entrances and tumbled onto the stage to the James Bond theme. And that's who I was that day: Bond, James Bond.

But then, the worst. "Desperately needed for my talents" (unfortunately, flattery is a very strong motivator for me), was I game to take part in the fashion show where the finale would be the ever-popular "You Can Leave Your Hat On" routine from "The Full Monty"? All I had to do was strip down to my swim trunks. The true "full monty" (nude!) would not sit well with this five-star ship crowd.

By the time I found out this horrifying information (appearing in public with my shirt off) it was too late to make my escape i.e. jump overboard, OD on seasickness tablets, fake my own death...

Plus, the show had to go on.

"Come on, Mike", I coached myself, "You're only stripping for men and women old enough to be your grandparents."

I was so relieved and proud of myself. I did my little act and the whole thing went by in a blur.

Literally!

I merely took off my glasses and didn't see a thing: no faces, none of my fellow strippers, NOTHING within the surrealism that ship life can sometimes be.

Chapter 8:

BIRDS

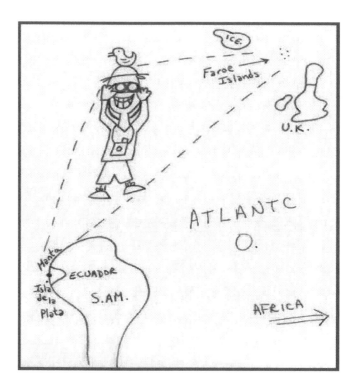

OK. Is this the regular treecreeper I'm looking at or the short-toed treecreeper?…

I started watching birds when on safari in Africa. A total accident, I quickly became addicted. How great is a hobby that you can do anywhere, be outside, and have access to unlimited information through the internet or countless guide books? The bag I carried on an escorted tour with camera, sunscreen, and notepaper also included bird book and binoculars.

Most of my birding had been with other people. Very inexperienced, I needed help with identifications, plus, I liked to glean information from experts. In Europe, I pretty much had only myself to count on, but this was good for my "training". I only counted a bird for my list if absolutely sure of its identity, having looked at all of its field marks and taken a photo, if possible. I did pretty well and became much more confident with my birding skills.

Many folks lovingly made fun of me for my nerdy little hobby. Some of the girls in my cast would come back from a day of retail therapy spouting, "Oh, Mike! We saw a BIRD today. We thought of you." I'd play along and ask what it looked like, whereupon they'd reply, "It was brown and it flew". Surely, these are the future authors of guidebooks.

During a cross-dressing party on the ship, a female friend and I went as each other. She wore my shorts, tie-dyed shirt, sandals, baseball cap, and had my binoculars around her neck for the whole evening.

Sharon in the Shore Excursion office would call me up and tell me to hurry in with my birding book. She had seen something unique and wanted to know what it was. I also had the cruise staff office on my side. They would be getting to know passengers and if somebody mentioned an affinity for birds, they would learn about me. I got to know quite a few enthusiasts this way, especially handy in South America. This trip was a one-shot deal; if there was something good to see, it had to be done right then.

Approaching Manta, Ecuador, I learned of La Isla de la Plata. I found a group of four that wanted to venture out with me on the long trip.

Our journey to the little beach town where we caught our boat was full of interesting sights. A donkey cart hauled a huge load of unripe bananas. We passed many basic homes, some built with simple slabs of wood coated with straw and dung. I had seen such homes in Kenya with the Masai people, but had no idea that dung was used here, as well.

At the crowded and touristy Punta Lopez, we paid our money and boarded our little vessel. An abundant supply of brown pelicans lived in the harbor and we also admired magnificent frigate birds. I knew them right away even without consulting my guide because one of the frigates displayed its red throat sac--very exciting! (But a subdued "exciting". People not into birds find the constant, "Oh, look!"s and "Wow!"s quite tiresome.)

Our trip over to the island was quite lengthy, as well, but worth it. I immediately found a bunch of new birds! Our guide, Winston, knew all of the Latin names for them, very wise! Hosting and guiding birders from all over the world, he couldn't possibly speak the entire melting pot of languages. By knowing the Latin names of the birds, he served everyone. Most guidebooks have the Latin names printed alongside the native speakers', so he proved extremely helpful. A frustrating point was that on one occasion, Winston only knew the local name for a bird. That did me no good, though, despite my efforts to identify it on the internet.

Blue-footed boobies living on the barren island waited. They settled everywhere, individual territories marked out around their nesting areas with dung. Each bird that we found, and its chick if it had one, remained in a white circle spattered onto the arid ground. We observed the chicks themselves in all stages of growth, some the size of their parent already and some barely out of the egg, shriveled like a dried out chicken wing. Was it dead? All of a sudden, its baggy neck would grotesquely stretch up and its avian eyes would take a peek at a strange new world.

Evolution worked right there on the island. In the Galapagos, the blue-footed boobies don't climb onto the low branches of the brush like those present on this island do. Can these birds not bear the excessive heat on those gorgeous azure feet?

We moved on. To see hundreds of magnificent frigate birds in their own protected nesting territory was an inspirational sight. The island also harbored three other kinds of boobies: the masked, red-footed and brown, but we didn't have the time, unfortunately, to walk those specific regions of the relatively small isle.

After reversing our boat and bus rides, we drove along the coast for the whole return trip, making it back with barely ten minutes to spare! I breathed a sigh of relief to cross the ship's threshold safely that day.

In the Faroe Islands, Danish territories found between Iceland and Scotland, I found myself on another birding excursion that involved a boat. A passenger initiated this trip and I signed up right away.

The trip to Vestmanna, one of the Faroe Islands, was rougher than that to Isla de la Plata with much colder weather. Rain gear helped us keep dry within our tossing little craft and once at our destination, we found a bit of shelter inside the giant geological masterpieces that the birds called home. Guillemots perched patiently on their nests, dangerously situated along sinister-looking cliffs that rose straight out of the wavy depths.

Puffins flew everywhere, their colorful beaks easily spotted. Traveling very close to the surface of the water, they beat their wings frenetically, producing a comical effect. We didn't see any puffin nests due to their frightening height way above us. Razorbills soared about, as well, but even if we did find their homes, I doubt that I would've been able to view their distinguishing bills through my very unsteady binoculars.

Solid ground much appreciated after this journey, the trip back to the ship was very green. The Faroes contained mini waterfalls everywhere, and sheep grazed impossibly along steep edges dropping right into the ocean. We marveled at their skill more than once.

My other birding excursions consisted simply of grabbing my bag of goods and searching about town for any park area harboring these surprisingly elusive creatures. Birds are heard singing, but nowhere to be found, teasing to be discovered somewhere within their perfect leafy perches.

Chapter 9:

SIDE DUTIES

Ten extra hours per week was our requirement onboard.

Pretty tough life, huh?

As entertainers, our hardest work was done off-sight during rehearsals, tediously learning and running the shows. Once that settled, our ship duties included manning the library, counting laps for "Walk-A-Thon", greeting people on the gangway in the morning, helping the tour staff dispatch tours, and the dreaded Captain's cocktail party.

This event entailed showing up to the ballroom and talking to as many guests as possible. More importantly, BEING SEEN talking to as many guests as possible. I realize that this isn't an unanaesthetized root canal, but the Caronia sailed with a lot of German passengers and a definite language barrier existed. Half of my energy was spent coolly hovering from table to table to determine who spoke what language in order to avoid embarrassment and awkward moments for all parties involved.

A self-important passenger once shooed me and my socializing partner away with a dismissive hand and scowl. Shocked, we quickly moved on, finding others who felt we were worthy of their time. This type of rejection did not happen often, but it would take me out of my dream-like state that I usually experienced at sea:

"I am getting paid to do this. This is NOT my vacation. All I have to do is dress properly, strike up some conversation, and follow a few rules."

The funniest "duty" that I ended up with was running the embroidery club on the Royal Viking Sun. Our itinerary consisted of long cruises on that ship. With all of the free time, I was working on a very involved cross-stitch project. Word got out about that one day when the social hostess was recruiting for help. Would I come by "Embroidery Club at 3:15 in the Evening Star Lounge with Cruise Hostess Yvonne" and help sort colors, tape edges, and get people started?

Sure! Why not?

This started as a mere one-time session, but I ended up RUNNING the thing! My NAME was even printed in the daily program a couple times. I hit the big time in cruise ship land! I did enjoy my forty-five minutes with the ladies every sea day, though, and it was good for me to be active rather than hibernating in my cabin.

The women entertained me during these "stitch and bitch" sessions; high school all over again:

"So and so was reported for not wearing a tie on formal night!"

" I wrote a strong letter to the head office regarding paper towel quality."

"Have you SEEN the way she dances with him??"

Passenger gossip ran amok, but at the same time, I felt like I helped people do something that they enjoyed and found relaxing.

The few guys present at Embroidery Club became my heroes. Some attended clearly because their wives talked them into it. Bless their hearts! I loved those guys, and smiled to see them with dainty needles in their big, rough hands.

But it was all about those ladies…

The most memorable gal was quite the curmudgeon. She floored me. As the girls discussed wedding photos one day, she piped in, "Why bother? You look at them once and then they sit on the shelf for years. Who cares?" She looked over at me, hoping for my approval, and added, "It's true".

Sometimes I played therapist. One woman volunteered her whole dysfunctional family history to me. Then I had a stitcher so insecure with herself that she insisted I watch her work for minutes at a time, to "make sure she was doing it right"! She'd come back the next time and repeat her whole ploy for attention. A German woman stitched and stitched because she was on a self-proclaimed mission to prove that those from her country worked hard! She completed three pillows in about two months and we all oohed and aahed her handiwork.

Mission accomplished.

My surrogate grandmothers/fathers developed into my unquestionable fan club for when I performed onstage. Most of the hoots and hollers I received were from my stitching cronies.

At the end of my contract, during our customary sherry party, I received a "Certificate of Merit and Appreciation" from them that they had all signed. I took a picture of the smiling, industrious group, proudly displaying their works, and remember them all fondly.

Chapter 10:

HEAVEN ON EARTH

Did you know that we only eat female bananas?

There is something for everyone in Costa Rica. The daring can bring out their inner Tarzan, harnessing up and cabling through the rain forest. Lean back for a faster ride! The quieter ones can hire a local to tour the banana plantations and shipping plants. We saw workers handling bunches that weighed up to ninety pounds! There are several beautiful beaches to partake in, as well, or reserves to go bird watching in. An impressive amount of Costa Rica's land has been set aside for conservation.

A couple of times, I went horseback riding. We were picked up at the ship and brought to a hacienda where our afternoon was spent traversing the gentle hills overlooking the harbor on beautiful caballos, very kind to us novices. I won't soon forget mounting a feisty horse and later galloping with him, an exhilaration of speed and wind tussling up my hair. Horses are such powerful, yet gentle creatures and in my limited experiences with them, I have always respected and appreciated their relationship to man.

After our ride, nature walks at the ranch and views of the lush valley awaited for those with any remaining strength. If lucky, a luxurious hammock could be enjoyed while waiting for the delicious FOOD!! Plantains are one of my favorite dishes in Costa Rica. Similar to bananas, but much heartier and less sweet, a tangy sauce served with them is their perfect complement.

Our itinerary had included a return to Costa Rica in a few weeks and the hacienda allowed us to reserve the horses for a much longer ride--four hours. This is quite a long time to straddle horses for below average riders, but we had enjoyed our short day and figured that the extended trip would be no problem...

By hour three, however, our leader, the guy who set up the trip, the man who bragged that he would have no problem riding for four hours, the man who wore BOXER SHORTS WHILE RIDING ON A HORSE, had to dismount his charge and humbly walk the rest of the way. By the end of the trip, even this was a problem for him (chafe, chafe) and the rest of us secretly chuckled at his deflated sense of machismo.

I have never seen such a startling case of saddle sore in my life. We are talking "scabs".

Unfortunately, my time in Costa Rica also includes the memory of having to leave one of my cast members behind with appendicitis. She was about to go to dinner, but could not get out of her bed due to the extreme pain in her abdomen. Before we sailed too far away from land, the doctor thankfully diagnosed her condition. The ship returned to the pier and discharged our girl into a waiting ambulance. She was very scared to be left in a foreign country, but English is widely spoken in Costa Rica with some of the best medical facilities in Central America. Her attack was actually timed quite well and she made a speedy recovery. She did not, however, return to the ship so we reblocked all of our shows to accommodate the change.

One of the best things I did in Costa Rica was visit a sloth rehabilitation center called Aviarios Del Caribe. NOT a twelve-step program for animals to recover from their substance abuse, these poor guys had been orphaned or injured. Sweeter creatures could not be met. They eat nothing but twigs and leaves, obtaining their water through the dewy flora they munch on, moving very groggily only AS IF in the midst of substance dependency.

We enjoyed seeing the tiny sloth babies, looking up at us with huge, innocent eyes. They looked like Ewoks. Buttercup is the star of the center. She's been on television and was a very good sport to let us all cuddle her and pose for photos. Her face's dark coloring around its edge gave the impression that she was sporting a sleek wig. The effect was quite comical.

Sloths' claws are something to be admired, long and useful in keeping them safe up in their arboreal dwellings. Their coarse fur is oily, their bodies very warm underneath it all.

I feel at home in Costa Rica. I can be the cowboy or the naturalist, depending on my mood. An appreciation for Mother Nature infuses the country and I respect that very much.

Chapter 11:

CHRISTMAS AT SEA

Santa Claus was very skinny that year…

I spent two Christmases at sea, very anxious because I consider the holiday a very important one for me to be with my family. However, I couldn't sacrifice six months of work and wonderful travel opportunities in order to be home for just one specific day.

Both Christmases busy with extra activities and caroling, little time remained for homesickness. In the Caribbean on the Royal Viking Sun, our tropical location was treat enough. This east coast boy had never had a warm Christmas and from St. Thomas on Christmas Eve, I called home. I also phoned my family from the ship on December 25 with a very expensive satellite connection. My brother shouted out that I sounded like I was underwater trying to communicate with him like we did as kids in our swimming pool! Nonetheless, it was special to connect with home for a few minutes and the crew ended up getting discounts for calls made that day.

We had a bit of a break later in the afternoon from rehearsing our Christmas show. Our backstage area was connected to a deck in the front of the ship and we stood out there enjoying some sun. All of a sudden, a huge pod of dolphins exploded out of the ocean! There had to be hundreds of them swimming along with us, jumping and frolicking in the waves. A few minutes later, the sight was enhanced when a rainbow materialized, our Christmas gift from Mother Nature!!

Within the cast, a Secret Santa gift exchange was underway. Everyone picked a name and bought presents for a person who would try to guess who their buyer was on Christmas morning. My Santa went to several people on the ship and had them write me a holiday note in their native tongue. The messages mysteriously arrived daily at my door with a small gift attached.

In the evening, we caroled around the ship for the passengers and did our "Home For the Holidays" show. At midnight, a completely different crew show was performed, making for a very full day.

My Christmas on the Caronia was very similar, except for departing from the Canary Islands on our way back to Southampton. I received a panicked phone call from the cruise director on Christmas Eve. His "Santa" had another commitment on Christmas morning, so would I be able to accept the challenge?

Now I am all for helping out, but hardly a jolly St. Nick-type!! "Skin-and-bones-Santa" was more like it, but it's amazing what a folded pillow and excited kids can do to complete the magical transformation. Santa did go over very well and giving the kids their gifts that morning was a treat.

My cast on this ship did a Secret Santa, as well, and everyone was shocked when their buyer was revealed! We had disguised ourselves well and ended that evening by performing a pantomime for the audience. A very British tradition during the holiday season, our "panto" was a unique experience. We played over-the-top characters, similar to those in a vaudeville show, in a thrown-together production of "Cinderella". Our audience loved it, knowing all of the parts where they had to join in with us and we greatly enjoyed performing something that was so different from our production shows.

Yes, I did miss two Christmases at home, but as I was wisely told, while fretting over feeling homesick, "Your holiday onboard is what you make of it". For those days, my shipmates became my family.

Chapter 12:

ZIGGY

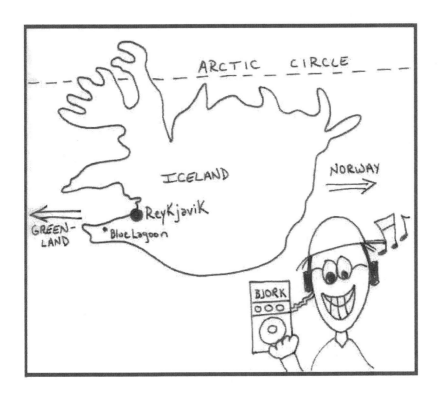

…"Do you eat puffins?"…

"Yes, yes." Ziggy giggles.

Our blonde guide is attentive to the curvy road and good-naturedly continues to answer all of my other questions, too.

"Are you from here?"

"Yes."

"What do you do for fun?"

He hesitates. I have embarrassed him.

"Do you like Bjork?"

"No!" He is very emphatic. "We can't stand her." I'm a bit shocked by this news, but Ziggy just laughs again.

My only background knowledge of Iceland is that Bjork, the strange pop music star, is from here. Unique Bjork. (Say that ten times!)

Anxiety fills me as we progress through the barren and endless fields and fields of sharp volcanic rock, black against a piercing blue sky. Boat drill was held this morning in Reykjavik. Horrible timing!

It took many days at sea to get here and since emergency-training drills need to be held every week for us, Reykjavik fell at the point on the calendar when drill was due. Standing around during drill and seeing this new landscape waiting for us was complete torture! Our time is very limited now.

Ziggy tells us that Iceland contains the world's northernmost capital. Homes and businesses are heated naturally with geothermal springs. Citizens pay one dollar per month for their heating bills! They do pay a lot of taxes, but their medical insurance is free. My mind wanders…

How long until we get to this place?

Will we have sufficient time to soak?

And can this guy's real name be "Ziggy"?

Once we had completed drill, my friends and I gathered out on the pier and cut a deal with a random van driver. He told us that his name was Ziggy, but perhaps his real name was wildly Icelandic, one that we couldn't possibly ever pronounce and he didn't have the patience to teach us. Oh, well. He's "Ziggy" to us today, a handsome local with a killer smile.

Somebody asks about the picture of the little blonde girl hanging off of his dashboard. She's his daughter, but he's not married. This lifestyle does not seem to be a stigma here like it can be in the States.

Moss-covered lava surrounds us as we snake along a road through what looks like a moonscape. A snow-capped volcano, hopefully dormant for today, juts out of the horizon. We learn that scientists use the DNA of Icelanders for genealogical studies—their stock is the purest IN THE WORLD!! Iceland's average life expectancy is topped only by Japan! All of this fresh cool air must pay off for the people here.

Finally!

Pure white steam from the belly of our planet has given away our arrival to the popular Blue Lagoon.

We pay our fee, don our swimwear, and indulge in the supposed healing qualities of the communal pool. How nice that our "activity" consists of just lounging around like great walruses, no rigorous exploring, no taking in of historical information required! The silica floating in the large swimming hole is whitish, but overall, looks like a milky baby blue. Once in the pool, silica mud is available in a bucket and we gleefully spread it on our faces and pale bodies, yet to see the sunny Mediterranean. When rinsed away, all of our dead skin is exfoliated off and we feel so, so nice and oh, so refreshed. Steam rooms and outdoor hot tubs are available, too, and we note that locals are regulars at the Blue Lagoon. Excellent news! We're not just the latest victims of a tourist trap.

My earlier worries are folly, as we had about two hours at the lagoon-- plenty of time in the powerful sun. I relish the shower that rinses away the grit and browse in the gift shop selling products so that this whole cleansing process can be relived in the bathtub at home.

While waiting for the girls, I ask Ziggy to say something in his native tongue. He plays along, but again, I've embarrassed the poor guy. What a good sport! He tells me not only that he speaks five languages (no surprise, being a typically multilingual European), but most impressively, Iceland has 100% literacy!

We are weary, riding away from the mystical-looking Blue Lagoon, brewing under all of that steam. It's a shame that we won't be able to see any of Reykjavik today, but I have a great excuse now to return. Maybe I'll escort the legendary Golden Circle tour someday that includes visits to geysers and loud waterfalls with fantastic names.

Iceland is more now than just "Bjork's homeland" to me. Hey, we met Ziggy! But will we ever see him again? Will he ever give Bjork another chance?

Chapter 13:

NEARLY NUDE PARTS II AND III: HAPPY NEW YEAR, MR. BEAR

Oh, the things I have done for "my art".

Imagine prancing about a five-star ship on December 31 wearing nothing but a diaper as Baby New Year! How nice of my fellow cast members to nominate me for the job, yes?

Midnight is tolling, I'm running all over and posing with everyone, and who calls me over to have a photo taken? Ernest Borgnine, HIMSELF! Now shouldn't that have been the other way around? Cruising as a passenger (rather than a guest entertainer) I chatted with him and his party for a bit...IN A DIAPER!

This just doesn't happen everyday.

And then there was dear ol' Mr. Bear. Mr. Bear and I had a long history together. In Magdelena Bay amongst the icy Norwegian fjords (in the middle of July!), the ship would always do this little "thing" where officers, the cruise director, and deck hands would set off in a tender to gather glacier ice that would be chopped up later and served onboard in cocktails. The boat was loaded up, its engine started, and the "explorers" motored out in search of the ice. Little did the passengers know that hidden onboard in a plastic bag was a brown bear suit. A male production singer/dancer (AKA me) would somehow "disappear" during the trip with a goofy brown theme park-like bear taking his place...

Around a corner and out of the ship's sight, I donned the crazy outfit (missing its left brown foot--funny how a sneaker-wearing bear was always caught). The tender then returned with an ice chunk and "savage" bear! Somebody gave me my "put up a struggle" cue and the deck hands thankfully mimed the prodding of the wretched beast, ripped out of its natural environment and brought into submission. Mr. Bear then got the net.

As the little boat was pullied back up onto the ship, with the Captain announcing our every move, the "bear" became docile, posing for photos or dancing with any folks willing to play the game. The gag always got a big laugh. Running into passengers later who winked knowingly and whispered how they'd figured out who was in the suit, I denied everything: "Oh, no! I missed it! I was watching a movie/napping/on the other side of the ship observing puffins..."

My last engagement as Mr. Bear was the most unique one. Ships usually stage an elaborate initiation system for passengers who cross the Equator or Arctic Circle for the first time. "King Neptune's" permission must be granted in order for them to cross and "sacrifices" must be made to him. This is usually the passengers' pride, in the form of spaghetti dumped on their heads, ice jammed down their swim suits, and smelly meringue gleefully smeared all over their bodies. To add insult to injury, the "victims" must also kiss a big malodorous fish that has been sitting in the hot sun all afternoon. THEN they must jump into the pool and clean off the junk. I suggest trying to be one of the first into the pool should you find yourself in this crazy line up.

During bad or cold weather, all of this was restaged indoors. Instead of the pool activities, silly, dignity depriving dances would be performed. Some did ballet and some did disco. The Chicken Dance and Macarena also made appearances. Last, but CERTAINLY not least, a group got "bear". The brown suit (still with no left foot) appeared on stage and its occupant started to gyrate a bit. Then slowly and seductively as possible in a bulky bear suit, the big hairy head came off.

Oh, look, there really IS a man under there!

I shimmied my way out of the suit, undoing the Velcro with as subtle a rip as I could manage and found myself, again on a five-star ship, in nothing but my skivvies.

One man was VERY into this and took his shirt off. I am so glad that alcohol wasn't involved in our little ceremony. I wiggled and jiggled a bit more and ran off, trying to maintain MY dignity.

Of course the ship's photographer was capturing this horror on film and of course she gave copies to the cruise director who immediately hung them up for all to see. A few days later, a couple cast members and I sat in the office laughing over them and a woman came in to ask a question, noticing the pictures of half-naked me.

"Oh," she said, "didn't he have a good bum? Look at those muscles!" I was a bit embarrassed, but we laughed about it even more, especially since this woman had no idea that, although the bum was all mine, I had painted the "muscles" on with make-up!

Chapter 14:

NUDE

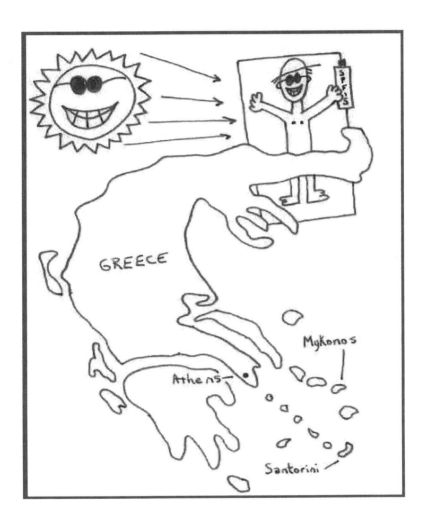

1) Being completely naked

2) Lying on a beach

Two of my favorite things added together equal the divine NUDE

BEACH EXPERIENCE!

My family used to vacation every summer on Martha's Vineyard. The beach we'd go to had "nudies" at the far end. My family never partook, but my young impressionable mind was very intrigued by this activity and I couldn't wait until I was old enough to try it for myself.

ENTER GREECE.

Now I am an all or nothing guy when it comes to getting naked. I can't stand having my shirt off, but let me be nude on a beach and I have no qualms whatsoever.

What does this mean?

I discovered a beach in Santorini, my first solo venture as a nudist. The driver of my bus and his friend just kind of laughed as I gingerly debarked at the stop I needed and nervously trekked to the shore. I didn't see anyone naked. Further down the coast, though, much more exposed skin glistened.

Relief!

It's always a walk to get nude. God forbid we show our stuff in a convenient location. I found my spot, spread my towel, took it all off and…

Ah. This was nice.

How freeing! How great to not have that elastic waistband leaving its hideous indentation on my skin. How nice to feel the sun where it had never been felt! How amazing to flop around in the water and not be paranoid that the bathing suit was falling down!

Once nude, there is no turning back.

Obsessed with my new discovery, I proceeded to visit every naked beach that I could find in Europe. Sunbathers of all shapes, sizes, ages, colors and disabilities go nude and it's wonderful. Nobody cares!

America is such a prudish nation. We freak out when a female breast is shown on television, yet don't even question the appearance of war dead on the news. In our natural states, financial worth and occupations are blissfully unknown. Obsessions with clothes and the impressions that they make are moot. Hallelujah!

I saw a guy at a beach on Mykonos. He walked along the shore, bare as the day he was born, speaking on a cell phone!

He must have felt naked without it.

Chapter 15:

DELICATE WINGS

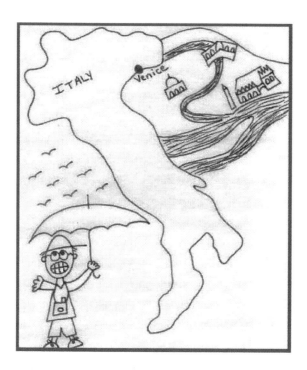

Venice, Italy just can't be real! It is a dream, some elaborate set for a Shakespeare play, not an actual lived in, historic city.

Viewing the sail-in to Venice is a must. I woke at 5 to witness the spooky time when fog reigns over the early morning and guide lights for the boats start to dimly appear. The sun wakes up, ever so gradually, and silhouettes of countless towers fade in. Mystical Venice appears, a surreal canvas with its muted colors and leaning structures. And this is just the sail-in!

Getting lost is a requisite. Even with a great map, I always fumble my way through the labyrinth that is Venice. I didn't run into anyone that I knew all day! Where is the ocean? In which direction is the Grand Canal? The more disoriented, the more I discover. I love being where no tourists are, yet also can't help loving San Marco Plaza and everyone there with their kids feeding pigeons! I find the sheer mass of birds pretty startling, but it's fun to see all of the happy little faces and I well up a bit thinking of me as a wee tot and how my Dad would've encouraged this behavior.

Modern day conveniences exist but don't belong in this medieval city. One moment I'm ogling crumbling paint and plaster, the next, reading signs for an internet café. Right behind a set of moldy steps leading into a canal, patrolled by a lone fish, is a tiny mechanic's garage and a discotheque!

A section of the canal has been marked off and drained for repair. I look down into the mess and see history's grimy layers. The place is crumbling to bits. A garbage barge is further down and just like any other city, I remember that Venice must be maintained.

It's utter joy to be a solo explorer. There are so many memories flooding back from when I was here during my college years. I had little money and slept in the train station! With my Eurail Pass, if a policeman bothered me, I explained that I was waiting for my train and was left alone.

The day is hot, but I find plenty of shade in a surprising park near the modern day ship-building area. It's lovely to buy my pizza, soft Babybel cheese, and piping hot bread, feeling completely gratified that I am much better off financially now than during my first visit.

The locals make Venice real for me; otherwise, I just can't put my mind around it. I bring my map and am lucky to find the glass animal-making man I had accidentally discovered during my last visit. He had been making bugs, but today he creates a butterfly, permitting me to stand in his shop for over an hour watching him. The only piece of his I can readily afford is a tiny snail. It's easy to imagine becoming his apprentice.

Continuing on my way, getting a nasty canal water whiff here and there, a woman struggles with her baby carriage over an angled bridge and I grab the front end for her. She thanks me profusely in Italian and just keeps speaking to me! I smile, realizing that I do that, too, in the States: "I know you can't understand me, but the more I enunciate and the louder I get, the better my native tongue will magically infuse itself into your brain." Ha!

Later, while another woman paints, a gust comes off of the sea and blows some of her work into a nearby canal, despite the attempts of many to assist her. Further along, the open doors of a mask shop welcome me in to watch artists create with papier-mâché, glaze, and gorgeous ribbons spread out on their worktables. Their wares hang on centuries-old exposed brick walls.

The hour is now late and the sky over San Marco Square an eerie yellow. A terrific storm is blowing in and I am alone.

Alone in San Marco Square! What a privilege this is! I can hear the ocean lapping loudly against empty gondolas. Perhaps the entire vast area will flood and the elevated walkways will be reassembled to keep everyone's toes dry. The floods cannot be good for Venice, but I want to see them. They are part of the city.

My shadow has never darkened the doorway of a museum or art gallery here. Too much else awaits outside whether a side trip to Murano for the glass-making factories, or a vaporetto (water taxi) to experience the Grand Canal view of Venice.

A few years later and without my map, I never find my glass animal-making man again. I try wandering, but my efforts are futile. Did I dream him up? Somebody is practicing their piano. The tune echoes down through the narrow alley as I recall those translucent creations with delicate wings.

Chapter 16:

WILDLIFE AT SEA

How improbable is a flying fish?

The powerful ship's prow slices through the ocean, creating a mesmerizing fountain, and all of a sudden, a gorgeous turquoise creature splashes out and sails over the undulating surface! And it flies quite a distance! After the journey, its strange wings fold back in and the fish crashes down, becoming aquatic once again. When caught, it's an oily, but delicious meal.

Many of my free hours were passed blissfully up on deck. Even with inclement weather, I just couldn't stay indoors all day. The fresh air at sea couldn't be beat and I took advantage of a schedule allowing me to read a great book or write postcards al fresco.

Binoculars always at my side, South America presented opportunities to view boobies, albatross, and petrels. But sea birds can be tough to identify because their unpredictable dipping and soaring make observation difficult in checking out their markings, and some just don't fly close by.

In the Iceland/Faroe Islands area, hundreds if not THOUSANDS of fulmars glided behind our ship. My skin actually crawled as I remembered Hitchcock's movie "The Birds". The little ghosts continued following us after sunset, too, floating and crying out from the absolute and chilling dark.

The Royal Viking Sun was unique in that the crew was allowed right onto the prow of the ship. My singing partner and I stepped into the gated area, literally spreading our arms and playing Kate and Leo in the movie "Titanic", when all of a sudden, a whole school of dolphins leapt towards us! They played in the wake for quite a few minutes as we jealously watched and admired their grace.

In Gibraltar, my guide on a dolphin tour very knowingly informed us that plain pictures of the water are the most common souvenirs from the trip. Those dolphins just move too quickly for our inept fingers to press that shutter release in time. I was a smarty, though, and thought I'd prove the guide wrong. I was lucky, but only because I never wasted film. I had entered the Digital Age. The majority of my perfectly framed pictures of waves got eliminated with one glorious button: delete.

Without a doubt, whales constitute the most spectacular wildlife at sea. Their "blow" is more often viewed than their grand bodies, each species of whale having specific spray patterns, differing in height, shape and frequency! The captain would always try to let the passengers know when a whale was nearby and if possible, slow or even stop the ship for maximum viewing pleasure. Sailing out of Juneau, Alaska one evening at the end of the summer season, I could hardly believe my eyes when I saw hundreds of humpbacks in their migration, spraying and diving. A baby whale was learning how to breach, too, the perfect setting for my dinner!

And in Hawaii, my friends and I had just finished swimming and I was all dried off and ready to go when informed that whales could be heard underwater! My friends had to be pulling my leg, I thought, but I reluctantly returned to the ocean, ducked my head under, and listened to the whale song, clear as an audiotape! They had to be miles and miles away, but the salty water provided perfect acoustics, well worth getting back into the ocean for.

Later, sailing away while I photographed a perfect rainbow hanging along the emerald coastline, some whales frolicked off in the distance. Could these have been the same ones I had been listening to, allowing me once again the privilege of their company?

Chapter 17:

HAINES, ALASKA...ALMOST

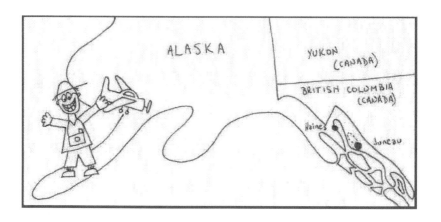

One day in Alaska, my stage manager told me he needed to amass flying hours towards his pilots' license. He was renting a plane in Juneau. Did I want to fly with him to nearby Haines as he continued fulfilling his requirement?

How could I turn down such an awesome experience? I eagerly expressed my interest. Another colleague had just taken the flight and enjoyed the trip to tiny Haines very much. I anticipated the views of Alaska from above, the thrill of a flight in a little plane.

Our day arrived overcast.

Hm...

We boarded a local bus to the (no lie) Nugget Mall anyway and from there, taxied to the airport. Paperwork complete, we entered the airstrip area to check the plane.

Oh, my word.

The plane was so small that it had to be TIED DOWN to the ground so that a gust of wind wouldn't flip it. Standing right in front of it, the top of my head came right to the top of the wing! After dealing with the initial shock, my excitement built.

My pilot, the man who held my life in his hands, untied the plane and we stepped in, just one seat for the each of us, plus a little bit of storage space for a cotton ball. I buckled up as the mandatory check-in was completed with the air traffic controller. It was pretty cool, the unseen voice of God. Mr. Pilot then turned to me and said, "Now don't be alarmed, but I have to go through crash procedures with you. It's part of the checklist."

So...

I inhaled deeply as he took me through all of that: how to tuck my head, keep my seatbelt on, pray, etc. He then went outside and literally, all kidding aside, TURNED THE PLANE'S PROPELLER WITH HIS HANDS to get it started! It's a wonder that I didn't bolt right then and there, but my legs had lost their feeling, circulation cut off at the point my knees imbedded into the dashboard.

His headphones and the roar that the little plane managed to produce prevented any chat time, but I was happy to just sit back, enjoy the flight, and let him do his work. On the runway, it started to rain.

Drat. NOT a good sign.

We took off nonetheless. Soaring down along the huge bay that Juneau is sprawled up to, the weather was closing in fast on our pretty view. Visibility quickly lessened and after only a few minutes, the plane had to be turned around.

There was nothing to be done but enjoy my circle tour of rainy Juneau. And we had the smoothest landing that I have ever experienced in ANY plane. I felt nothing!

A couple more times, I did fly from Juneau, but not with my stage manager. Crew tours to a nearby island known for bear sightings were offered with a mama bear and her three adorable cubs as the highlight and floatplanes toured over nearby glaciers. Their operators gave generous crew discounts at season's end.

I enjoyed the chance to take off from and land in the middle of the bay. Though spectacular, these flights did not compare with the novelty of my private puddle jumper.

Chapter 18

TOUR ESCORT HELL

"One passenger is still missing, and we've been waiting for almost an hour!"

This is a tour escort's nightmare, my nightmare. The day had started out so nicely…

The Shore Excursion office onboard always needs to have somebody on every bus dispatched to help the guide count passengers. A form is filled out for every tour that reports problems, too. Escorts enjoy the sights and the tour costs them nothing, a win/win situation for all involved. Most of these tours are marvelous experiences, but this one is souring fast.

Docked in Warnemunde, Germany, my group bussed to Berlin for an all-day tour. The trip there alone lasted three hours, but despite our limited time, we managed to see a lot of sights. Charlottenberg Castle became our first stop on the edge of town; we drove by Checkpoint Charlie, and visited remnants of the horrid wall that my guide actually helped dismantle with a hammer kept in her kitchen! The magnificent Reichstag was next before our buffet lunch at a local restaurant. We drove around Berlin visually sampling its modern architecture and museums. A mental note has been made that this fantastic city is one to come back to.

Culminating at the Brandenberg Gate, our tour itinerary allowed for a small amount of time on our own to shop, use the facilities, and return to the bus for the long journey back. Our guide could not have been clearer in explaining the location of the rest rooms within a nearby shopping center and everyone made it back on time.

Except this one.

Only one.

AAAAGGGGHHHHHH!!!!!!!!!

"Does anyone know who this person is?"

A basic description quickly established, an "elderly man with a cane, wearing a white baseball cap" was diligently hunted for. Nobody knew what his plans had been during the break, but he was seen in the shopping center. OK. Our guide went to look for him. The four other buses from the ship on this tour have all left us now and my group is just sitting while we wait for this man. Under normal circumstances, we only wait for someone who is tardy for about fifteen minutes and then let them find their way back to the ship by cab. But we're in BERLIN, an enormous metropolitan area three hours away!

I'm most worried over whether this missing man had a heart attack or something. Our tour dispatcher is back in the mall now checking bathrooms and making announcements on the loudspeaker!

I really hope that works.

I ran over to the shopping center a couple of times myself to see if I could find this guy wandering around aimlessly.

No luck with anything…

We have GOT to leave him. We've been waiting for an hour now. This is unheard of and the time in limbo for everyone else on the bus is unfair. Our tour dispatcher has left himself behind to continue the seemingly fruitless search and figure out what to do.

What has happened to our poor guy?

Is he dead?

Kidnapped?

Suffering from a sudden bout of amnesia?

We are leaving this elderly man behind in a crowded city where he doesn't speak a lick of the language and the ship is THREE HOURS AWAY, sailing tonight.

There is nothing I can do…

…We're about halfway through our trip now, and amazingly enough, our guide has just woken us up to announce that a speeding cab has approached our bus, containing our "missing" man! I CANNOT believe this, but he's wearing the telltale white baseball cap! I am so relieved, but people are already grumbling that we're stopping so that he can rejoin us! They want him to cab the whole way back! Mutiny is brewing and it doesn't smell pretty.

Stomachs are rumbling and the passengers must, they MUST, get to their awaiting dinners onboard. Many unhappy folks on my bus would rather hear that this man has suffered from a heart attack while buying bits of the Berlin Wall than allow him to reboard and just forget this mess.

Pulling over for the cab, we sit here waiting for Mr. Man, but rather than making a humble and speedy trip over to our vehicle, this guy has hobbled out of his cab to pee in front of us all! The women are gasping and the men (including myself) are quite incredulous over his audacity! Could he not have found some kind, ANY kind of barrier? Speaking of the Berlin Wall…

To make things worse, this man has taken his seat on the bus and given NO APOLOGY whatsoever! THIS is what shocks me. I personally don't care what happened, but the man has no idea how much he has inconvenienced us. I am, however, getting a huge kick out of the complete exasperation he's causing all of these rather uptight people.

I'm just trying to enjoy the rest of the ride now. Instead, one by one, seething passengers are coming to visit me in the back of the bus:

"Well, you're in charge, make him apologize!"

"First of all, lady, I am NOT in charge. I am merely an innocent escort wishing I had stayed in "BLOODY" Warnemunde all day."

Next in line is an overweight man who looks as if he's going to burst a blood vessel on his ruddy, bulbous neck. (POINTING his finger at me): "Are we going to miss dinner? If I miss my dinner…" (His lower lip juts forth and he shakes his head threateningly.)

"No, sir, the ship has been informed of our tardiness and dinner will be held for you. Looks like you wouldn't suffer much from a missed meal anyway."

These people turn into children right before my eyes. It's magic. Yes, this man was careless to get lost. Yes, this man was wrong to not apologize. He'll probably demand that Cunard pay for his cab, too (he did, they didn't) but for God's sake, it's not the end of the world. Can we please move on?

Finally, Clueless Missing Man realizes that he has caused quite a stir and his fellow bus mates are preparing to lynch him. He turns around and feebly says to the awaiting crowd, "I am deeply sorry for any problems I have caused".

Great.

That's nice. He means it.

This makes for a funny story now that we can just tell our friends. Right?

No.

A grown woman, old enough to be a grandmother, yells out, "You've wasted an hour of our lives!"

I'm going to bury my head now and finish filling out my report.

Chapter 19:

TOUR ESCORT HEAVEN

The Shore Excursion Manager looks to his left.

He looks to his right.

On the streets of Madeira, Portugal, an island known for its adventurous downhill basket rides, I have just come out of the internet café. Nobody else from the ship can be seen. He approaches and leans in to me, whispering conspiratorially, "Mike, do you want to go to Machu

Picchu?"…

A month previous, another cruise is ending. The ship is abuzz with activity as final paperwork is done, borrowed library books are returned, and business cards exchanged. Five flights up lead me to the deck housing the cruise director's office containing the production casts' mailbox. New escort forms for the upcoming South America cruise are available. We will circle the entire continent over fifty-eight days and the tours being offered are fantastic. I check off a bunch that I am interested in and as a joke, laughing as I do so, I mark my interest in the very expensive and exclusive Antarctica flight-seeing trip AND the three-day long Big Mama: Machu Picchu. Everybody wants to escort these trips, but we know that only the Shorex staff gets to go. South America is so rich with excursions, though, we'll all have our share of great experiences…

…I almost fell over!

DID I WANT TO GO TO MACHU PICCHU? You bet your Chocolate Midnight Buffet, I do!

Honored that they would ask me, I had to gain clearance from my Cruise Director first. He had scheduled programs for the two nights I'd be gone that involved the cast, but not necessarily me as they were variety shows. I was grateful for his flexibility in allowing me to go.

Now I was paranoid about other crewmembers (and even the Captain's wife!!) that had wanted to go. What was so advantageous for me was my open schedule; everyone else was working regular office hours. I was very lucky. Nobody keelhauled or fed me to the sharks, but I bet some wanted to.

The tour went out with over one hundred passengers, so that is why I was "needed". Honestly, I did nothing. The flight to Cuzco from Lima, Peru was so well organized, the tour company so well staffed, that I was basically there to enjoy yet another amazing free trip. I counted everybody twice during the whole three days, but did have the big job of gathering passports when we returned and delivering them back to the Documentation Officer.

This made me nervous. I could just see it. I'm crossing the threshold of the gangway onto the ship and drop my pile of passports into the soup, effectively stranding us all in Peru: "That useless idiot of an escort!"

Luckily, this scenario came nowhere close to happening, but I trembled visibly with my precious cargo.

I lost my breath in Cuzco. My room (I had my OWN ROOM!) was five floors up and impatient with the elevator, I scrambled up the stairs and became completely winded! What a surprise! Was I not working hard enough during my shows? I was flabbergasted, never having experienced that before. Then I remembered our altitude. Ah, yes. My ego rested.

Our first day in Cuzco was a preview to the grandeur of Machu Picchu. We arose on the second day, had an early breakfast, and boarded our train for the three-hour trip. In between "oohs" and "aahs", a very sweet woman told me how she fell in love with her husband while they bicycled across Europe! What a time! She was very careful to stress that although it was just the two of them together, he was always a gentleman. From the town of Aguas Calientes (our penultimate destination), we bussed up to the Incan city of Machu Picchu itself.

I always find it surreal to finally see with my own eyes that which I have spent my life looking at either on film or in photographs. Am I looking at the real thing this time? Machu Picchu looked the same as I had imagined, like the Mona Lisa, the Grand Canyon, or the Eiffel Tower. No surprises, so I focused on the details. How was the specific lighting affecting the place? What smells caught my attention? How did the air feel? My visual element of surprise diminished, the other senses had to kick in to make the experience "real" for me.

I stuck with my little group for the first two hours. I wanted to hear as much info as I could, but also had to do some hiking. Time was running out.

After capturing the most popular view on my camera, I flew across the whole city to leave the grounds and start the auxiliary climb up the sugar loaf that's always seen in the background of any Machu Picchu shot.

Climbing and climbing.

Sweating.

Resting, taking photos at different angles, and at different viewpoints, I looked up one last time and saw I was nowhere near the top. I was not going to make it.

I had to surrender to the clock and crawl back down.

Our visit to Machu Picchu lasted four hours. Many other lesser-known ruined cities hide along the great Inca Trail. I must revisit someday with a guide, camping in the jungle and waking up to the varied sounds of birds.

This visit was just a nibble, but so delicious.

Chapter 20:

SIDEWALK STAR

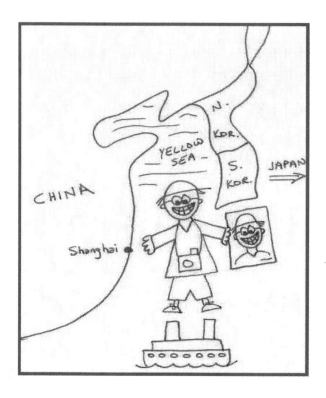

Mingzu pulls out his well-worn pencil and gets busy. For the equivalent of $1.25, he sketches my portrait.

In Shanghai, China, I have just discovered a couple of ancient temples whose ages I can't even fathom. A man on the congested streets offers to do my portrait for nine yuan. I have never done this, so, why not?

Within minutes, a large curious crowd of people has gathered around me. I cannot believe the stir that I am creating. Personally, I enjoy watching people sit to get their portraits done, and have wondered what it must be like for the models to see their onlookers judging the work as its created.

Several Chinese faces look at me and then switch back to Mingzu's work, most nodding in appreciation, but one woman is quite disapproving. She shakes her head with vehemence and clicks her tongue, making me very nervous.

I sit and concentrate as my man sketches, refines, and blends. How long do I have to smile? My mouth tires and I feel an artificiality slipping in. I remember that Miss Americas will put Vaseline on their teeth so that their lips won't stick to them. This makes sense to me now.

Finally, the big moment arrives and Mingzu turns around his pad for me.

Hey!

Not bad!

I am quite impressed. I can see a resemblance to my DAD! Now THAT'S talent!

One man asks if I am French (huh?) and a couple girls ask if I'm from California (why that particular state?). I do not understand what this question implies until somebody on my ship explains. These girls must've thought that I looked like I was from Hollywood! Ha! I have to laugh, but I was an American on display and perhaps the stereotype in China is that all young-looking Americans are movie stars. Who knows?

I have a great time showing off my portrait and hearing from everyone what they think. The surprising consensus is that it looks nothing like me! Just how do people see me? Maybe the mouth is a little off, but looking at the nose up, I think the drawing is a very accurate likeness.

Nonetheless, for this one day (or, OK, thirty minutes at most) I had become the Hollywood star that I had always fantasized about being.

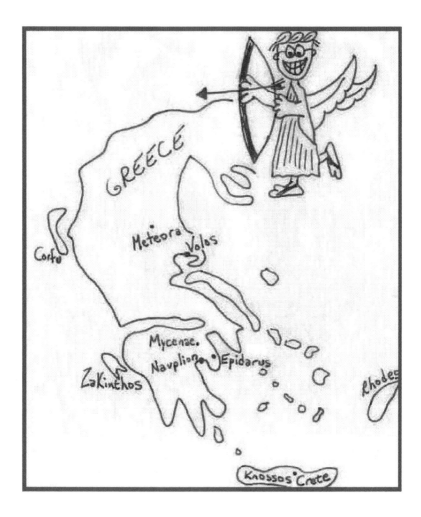

The air of late summer rattles with cicadas. Their sound makes me homesick. Strangely, I am longing for my childhood. I have never associated them with my past before, but maybe they remind me of an ancient past, inherited many generations over through my DNA. I am, after all, in Greece.

Knossos is my destination today. This Cretan palace housed Ariadne, who fell in love with Theseus, thrown down into the famous labyrinth to kill the horrible minotaur. I read the tale as a kid and loved all of the other mythological stories, too. I anxiously search the complicated depths of these ruins for the maze, long since gone. It is hard to believe that one of my favorite myths originated right here. The cicadas continue to perform the same song that they did in those days, too. Have they mesmerized me?

I am awed with this country and the corrosive passage of time.

Next is a visit to Mycenae, near Navplion. I knew all of the tales associated with this once grand palace. Stately Clytemnestra, a woman of such power in her day, now lies who knows where? Her honeycomb grave of porous limestone haunts me as I enter the cavernous space from the intimidating canyon leading into it. Where, too, is the great Agamemnon, her husband? His gold funeral mask lies in an Athens museum now. Imagine discovering that!

Feeling very daring after bussing back to Navplion, I take an afternoon trip to the well-preserved theatre in Epidaurus. An impressive sight, this theatre has to be one of the best examples left from the ancient Greeks. The acoustics really are perfect. I am not bold enough to step up onto the stage and start singing, but two young boys are immodestly playing air guitar and I can hear their every word and strum from all the way up in the last row! The stones I sit on look as if they are solid algae. From a nearby forest, the blistering sun has cooked oil from the pine trees, the aroma wafting over my nose as the cicadas start their concert again. A vendor sells cheese phyllos, perfect to tide me over for the trip back.

Almost as mythological as Mycenae is the city of Rhodes, once home of the famous Colossus, another seventh of the original Ancient Wonders of the World. The bronze statue is long gone, but I can imagine its scope. Was it really big enough in those ancient days for a ship to sail through its legs? I am skeptical about that. Entering the city wall, I chuckle over how much Rhodes has grown since its construction! The walled section is a mere neighborhood now. A woman deftly knots a silk carpet. I could admire her skillful weaving all day. The intensely fine work seems much more difficult to achieve than that of the wool carpet maker. This piece is glowing.

Meteora is a day trip away from Volos. Quite "modern" in comparison to everything else I have discovered in Greece, its main attraction is of mythological proportion. Monks ingeniously built their monasteries on steep outcroppings, having to use pulleys in order to cart all materials, plus themselves, up to the dizzying apexes. Many of these buildings existed in their prime, where now only about ten remain. But what efforts! Just how persecuted were these monks to have had to go to such extremes for their religion? From afar, the stone buildings look as if they are floating on top of delicate sand castle drippings, ready to collapse at any moment. Swallows teem in the air, nesting in the abundant crevices. Meteora has long since become tourist friendly— bridges lead to most of the monasteries now, but a few dangerous looking pulleys still remain. These monks risked their lives every time they left the safety of their perches.

One of the most heart breaking sculptures I have ever seen awaits in Corfu's Achillian. This entire estate is a tribute to the great Trojan War hero, Achilles. Outside in the garden lies "Dying Achilles". He has just received the fatal arrow in his heel, his body writhing in agony. The whole story is laid right out in stone through that one moment. I am awed by its perfection.

Finally, in Zakinthos, I have decided to hike. The cicadas have struck up their loud chorus. More and more of the city and port come into view as I continue my upward climb. I pass a pine tree oozing sap and finally understand how amber forms. The fortress I end up at contains young olive trees with their beautiful silver leaves, the same which made up the crowns for the winners of the nascent Olympics, that offered Noah a promise delivered by his dove, and those used to cover nude bodies during our prudish phases of civilization. I examine the humble leaves for quite a while.

I am in Greece. I am finally in Greece. It is difficult to absorb everything that I have seen here. Besides the vegetation, I could be back in upstate New York during a hot summer. How is this land the birthplace of all those myths? What made this land so special?

The cicadas are still rattling.

Chapter 22:

A LETTER TO BARB

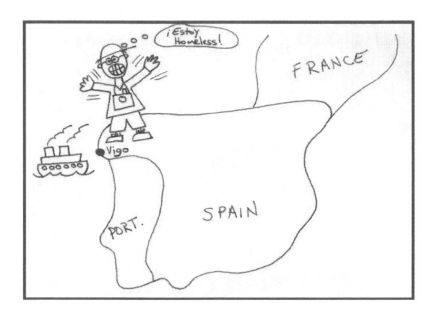

My friend Barb and I consistently e-mailed each other during my time at sea and this letter is pretty much word for word what I wrote to her that day...

OH MY GOD.

I have to tell you about my adventure in Vigo, Spain. Barb, I pray this never happens again, my worst nightmare came true.

I MISSED THE SHIP TODAY!! I watched the Caronia sail away from the dock and I WAS NOT ON IT! Of course, this all had to do with a nude beach.

Let me explain.

I found out that these really neat looking islands off the coast of Vigo, Spain have a regular ferry that goes over to them and there are great beaches, including a nudie one. So we dock in Vigo and I catch the 11:00 ferry. I know that I HAVE to catch the 2:00 PM ferry back so I can reboard the Caronia at 3:30 for our 4:00 sail away.

Dandy.

I board the ferry, endure the nauseating trip (this never happens to me) and end up at one of Las Islas Cies. I can't wait to explore this paradise right outside the very bustling city of Vigo and now want to take a separate vacation there, just so I can spend more time on these gorgeous islands!

Pine forests border the beach and although I didn't take my binoculars, I enjoyed the birdsong. I probably would've spotted some new birds because I don't get the chance to see many pine forests at our stops. My sense of adventure is very well piqued and I find the beach, strip, and just enjoy the peace, surf, and glorious sunshine. I figure that I have to leave at 1:45 to get the ferry back, so I do just that, lollygagging back all happy and satisfied. My clock says 1:55 and I get within sight of the dock to see the ferry LEAVING without me!!! My clock was off by 10 minutes!! The ferry left 5 minutes late and I still missed it.

OH.

MY.

GOD!!!!!!!!!!!

The horror, Barb, the shear and absolute horror. The next ferry is at 6 and the Caronia leaves at 4! I am totally out of luck. But, strangely, I didn't panic. My "If only…" voice was working full time, though, and THIS was awful.

I went to the restaurant at the dock and met this nice guy, Lucas, who totally saved me. First he told me to ask the Red Cross people if they had an extra boat to take me back! Their answer was a resounding, "¡No!"

Lucas then let me use his phone to call the port agent. I had taken my daily program from the ship with me, which I never do. It had the number in there that I needed and I happened to have a LOT of money on me which is never the case, either. I finally get through to the port agent and the "very helpful" woman there tells me, "You know the ship won't wait for you."

DUH, I know that, but can you please just tell them I will be late???!!!!!

The restaurant owner next calls a friend to see if he can come pick me up.

Tick tock tick tock.

The friend can't make it.

Next scene: Me, The Reigning International Ass, out on the pier yelling out to all the boating vacationers and asking in horrible Spanglish if someone can return me to Vigo! "I have money", see. A few of them did look over to me, but I was rightfully ignored otherwise. Ha, that dumb-ass American missed his ferry! Who cares? He can get the one at 6, right? So now I am beginning to do the whole, "Well, I will have to catch a train to Lisbon (our next port)/I may lose my job/at least I have my credit card, so I guess I'll be OK."

Barb, I can't believe I didn't just lose it.

So I go back to Lucas and discover that the restaurant owner has called another friend of his. It is 2:30 now and I have to be back on the Caronia at 4. The ferry took 40 minutes to go from Vigo to this island and I am starting to bigtime worry. BUT...

The other friend can come for me! It will take only 20 minutes to get here. It is now 2:55.

20 minutes…

20 minutes…

3:15 and there is still NO sign of this guy.

NO SIGN AT ALL.

I thought that maybe these guys were just pulling my leg and having fun with me. This is the point where I looked at Lucas and I said, "I am not going to make it." I completely surrendered. It was an amazing calm.

I should know by now that when I surrendered I was saved because this happens to me ALL THE TIME. I let it go and then it came to me.

Suddenly, racing and bouncing around like a stuntman in a great movie chase, this tiny boat sped closer! It was a very windy day and struggling to get to me, he finally reached the pier. I jumped onto the little speedboat at 3:25 and we zoomed right out of there.

THE SHIP LEAVES AT 4:OO!

It was an extremely bumpy and very, very wet ride. I ended up soaked and my lower back killed me for days after. My driver kept yelling MUCHAS OLAS. Many waves. And he wasn't lying. We are racing, racing, wet, wet.

I can see Caronia getting bigger and bigger, but so slowly. Hope is rising when we COMPLETELY stall, the engine waterlogged. OH MY GOD AGAIN!!!! I could NOT believe this!! We are floating there helplessly and he is struggling to start the thing up again.

Tick, tock, tick, tock.

God. So close and I am still going to miss this ship. I have to PAY this guy, too.

Finally, it starts up again and we get to the pier, but he can't find a place for me to get off safely because it is so windy. In the meantime, I grab my bag and give him ALL MY MONEY, which is 35 euros and 12 dollars, and tell him in bad Spanish ES TODO MI DINERO TENGO. It is all the money I have. The guys back on the island had said it would be 50 euros, so I was short, but this guy didn't even count the soggy money. He is my angel. I even repeated over and over to him, MI ANGEL, MI ANGEL. My angel, my angel. He had to think I was bonkers, but he truly was my savior and I kept apologizing for his being soaked, LO SIENTO LO SIENTO, but he brushed that off, too. He was very kind, he did NOT even have to help me. God, I was so lucky.

I race to the gangway of Caronia that is, of course, packed away. It is 4:00 on the button. I see the Captain up on the bridge looking down at me, no door open to jump back onto the ship and I am just dying at this point. But then, the port agent scrambles over to me and informs me that I have to go BACK from where I ran and catch the pilot.

THE PILOT!!

I had completely forgotten about the pilot!!!!!!!! The ship always has to be escorted out of the dock area by the local pilot up in the bridge and then a boat comes to take HIM back to the shore, so I was able to catch that boat and be brought back to the Caronia in that manner. In fact, the pilot boat captain had been yelling at me to stop running and join him when I debarked the speedboat, but in my panic, I had run right past him.

I get onto THIS boat and explain to the man (badly of course) that I have no money left to give him. He explains that it is his job to pick up the pilot and I don't owe any more money to anyone. So there I was, able to relax a bit, watching the Caronia pull out without me. HOLY CRAP, BARB, HOLY CRAP!!! Wet, exhausted, relieved.

HUNGRY!

I take a photo of the Caronia pulling away, a rare shot. Your ship is leaving and you are not on it. We get closer and I thankfully realize that because I called the port agent and reported I'd be late, a ship-wide announcement would NOT have been made for me, so nobody would know that this had even happened. I was very grateful, but embarrassed now, too. I looked up onto the deck as we approached the ship and saw 3 of the office staff looking down at me laughing and waving. I knew then that this wasn't going to be so bad.

Closer and closer to the ship, there was still no door open for me. I ask, again badly, where the door is and the driver just says he's going to get the pilot.

HUH??

All of a sudden, a door opens that is 2 stories above water and a rope LADDER comes rolling out that I have to climb!!!!! I had to climb this ladder UP THE SIDE OF A MOVING SHIP to reboard Caronia!

OH MY GOD YET AGAIN!

As I'm doing this, my hat blows off, and I go back down to rescue it before it becomes a permanent part of Vigo's waters. Then I make my final ascent up the steel walls. The safety officer and deck staff are there all smiles and "Ha-ha"s and the first thing Mr. Safety Officer does is take away my boarding card. I figured that that would happen. He said he'd let me know what the staff captain wanted to do with me.

Dum duh dum dum...

I am soaked.

I am cold.

I am humbled.

It was 4:15 when I got back onboard the ship. I strip (again!!), shower, and head up to the cruise director's office to share my tale with everyone. They were all impressed that I called the port agent. The CAPTAIN had called the office to ask if he should hold the ship for me and was told "no"! If I was resourceful enough to call the port agent, the office figured that I could make my way to Lisbon. Plus, there wasn't a production show that night. HALF of me understood that, but I had only needed a few minutes more! The ship could've waited for me.

The safety officer meanwhile has come in to deliver the verdict that I will NOT get a written warning, but I do have to miss the next two port days: Lisbon and Gibraltar. Fine. I am so relieved I don't even CARE!! I have been to both ports many times. Besides, I am so into Wimbledon right now, I would have probably been inside watching the tennis matches anyhow.

Now that it's over, my big adventure in Vigo was an awesome experience. I discovered these fantastic islands, had a thrilling speedboat ride, and did all that I could've to help myself, catching the ship in the end as a BONUS! Many strangers helped me. That touched me most. Nobody had to do squat for me.

I have NEVER been more relieved to be back on the ship than I was today. I was so thrilled they could've honestly taken away my shore leave for the whole cruise. I'd've been fine.

Whew! Can you believe it? My worst nightmare came true today. I saw two boats that I needed leave without me.

Chapter 23:

INDIANA JONES HAS LEFT THE BUILDING

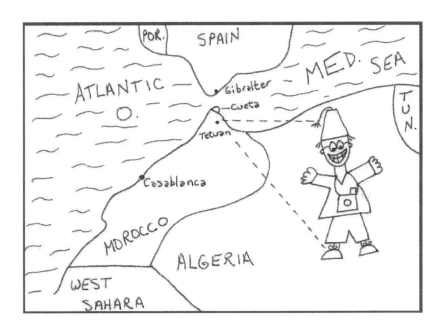

Until visiting Morocco, my vision of "Africa" was limited to "safariland" sub-Saharan Africa. A huge fan of the Indiana Jones movies while growing up, I didn't think of them as taking place in Africa because giraffes and elephants didn't roam around the background.

Spanish North Africa's city of Cueta, right across the strait from Gibraltar, bridges two continents, two significant bodies of water, and four cultures: Hebrew, Christian, Hindu, and Muslim. From Cueta, I toured into Tetuan, Morocco. The border crossing was a big deal, our passports required to be kept with us. I took delight in the camels at the side of the road, but learned from our guide that they are not indigenous to the area at all, there only for the benefit of tourists. Apparently, we Westerners think that we should see camels in any desert, so the

Moroccans provide.

Many guides accompanied us on this tour. Dressed all in white and wearing turbans, they appeared just like the men in the movies. A crowded city, Tetuan contained many homes whitewashed with paint that wards off mosquitoes. Our guides completely surrounded us as we disappeared into the dizzying market, or casbah, a twisting and dark labyrinth of short alleys and infinite corners housing impossible numbers of market stalls, each labeled with strange curvy writing. How could all of these people make profits?

Matching my guides, I tried on a lightweight outfit of linen along with a bright red fez. Bunnies sold at one market made me wonder, "Pets or food?" Chickens ran wild all over.

Exotic smells abounded—orange blossoms and tiger balm. Spices of all colors and aromas wafted in the air. Masses of children giggled and hid in corners, curious about all of the strange-looking white people wearing shorts and armed with cameras. Our guide, J'Mal, taught us how our numbers come from Arabia, how fifteen hundred words in English are Arabic in origin ("pajamas" being just one), and how there are two hundred words in his language for "lion"!

Everywhere, intricately carved wood was incorporated into architectural designs. The shapes of arches and windows differed greatly from the Greek and Roman influences that I was used to.

Taken into a carpet shop, sweet nana tea was served up, minty and surprisingly refreshing. The mint aids digestion and ironically, the heat keeps you cool. Not only shown every gorgeous carpet in stock, a demonstration of the local perfumes and spices unfolded. The "King of Spices", saffron, could be ours for a mere $96/ounce!

Everything was packaged very basically, requiring no glitzy boxes and ribbons, having been sold that way for thousands of years. The waxy, but pleasant cedar wood and jasmine cube I rubbed onto my arm (also used to discourage mosquitoes) came home with me in a simple plastic bag.

A lively bunch playing huge castanet-looking instruments and blowing long, thin horns greeted us for dinner. Some performers danced around and spun long tassels attached to their hats. Seated at low tables on comfortable pillows, course after course of delicious local food was served to us, including a colorful salad of onions, artichokes, tomatoes and olives. A belly dancer (who actually looked like she didn't want to be there) entertained us, along with singers, and a man who balanced a full tray of candles on his head, spinning around and never dropping a thing. The festive group of passengers that I sat with added to the pleasure of this meal.

What a full day, exposed to so much from this fascinating culture! Returning to our modern ship was a jarring contrast to the smells, stuffy heat, and variety of people that I had spent the day with. I felt as if I was in a trance for the rest of the night.

Chapter 24:

GROWN-UP IN MALTA

Every country seems to have "owned" Malta at one time or another during its tumultuous history. Now that things have settled down a bit for the tiny country, it makes for an interesting stop on the Venice, Italy and Dubrovnik, Croatia itinerary. Constructed from the same yellowish stone of the land, all of the island's buildings look as if they have sprouted directly from the earth.

The megaliths on Malta are some of the oldest stone structures in the world, incredibly pre-dating the pyramids in Egypt! The capital city of

Valletta is a great place to walk around and enjoy all of the different colored balconies that hang so precariously over the precisely straight streets.

One time in Malta, we had an overnight stay. Wandering around with a friend, our challenge of the day was to keep cool under the intense Maltese sun. Valletta does not support many trees, so we had to trek quite a distance to find shade in a little park overlooking the entrance to the port. The park also happened to be a former citadel, so we found ourselves in quite a grand setting: a faux Roman temple before us, a row of impressive columns behind that, and the flat, blue Mediterranean further behind. We sampled a local soft drink, Kinnie, in frozen form, and caught our breath for a few moments. A yellow and black-spotted ladybug landed on my leg, allowing us a photo shoot before flying away.

That night, as we readied for our scheduled show, a brilliant full moon rose over the town of Vittorioso across the long harbor. A lot of the crew planned to go to a club at the more modern town of St. Julian's, but that did not appeal to me. I was happy when a couple cast members expressed interest in walking around some more.

By the time we three climbed back into town, it was 11:30 at night. The barren streets felt haunted at this hour, with occasional street lamps and the moon our only illumination. Everything had settled. There was peace in the cool air. I like to imagine that ghosts play at this time; this stony, cobbled city full of fading balconies became the perfect setting for that fantasy to bloom.

We walked and walked, ready for a place to settle for a bit. We finally found this tiny bar and my friend managed with his best "Maltenglish" to fulfill his desire for a beer. I was ravenous by this time, and practically kissed his feet when he pulled out a bunch of bread pilfered from the crew mess. Ah. My other companion and I sipped wine.

Settling on top of a stairway leading to a bell tower, which was a popular tourist spot, we overlooked the dim harbor and saw not a soul. We dug into our snacks and talked about mortgages! Only one of us was able to talk from experience, but the other two expressed hopes of soon owning homes. We laughed about this, knowing that the rest of our cast was out dancing, none of them even remotely talking about such "grown-up" affairs. How nice to share this time with people who were on the same plane as me: unsatisfied to remain on the ship, but wanting to do something besides go to a crowded, smoky club.

Our bodies finally ran out of adrenaline. We climbed warily down our steps and returned to the ship through the silent, spooky streets.

Chapter 25:

RENEGADES PART I: THE FALKLAND ISLANDS

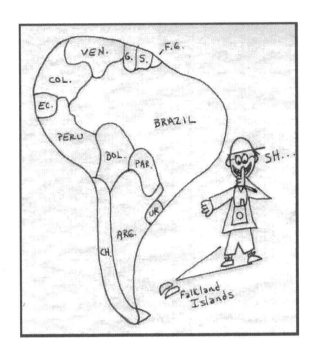

Call me "Mr. Goody Two-shoes".

I had straight A's in school and never cut class. I always follow the rules, except when desperate.

On the Royal Viking Sun's South America cruise, I missed the Falklands because my passport was in Brazil getting its visa. Besides, we had windy weather that day and by the afternoon, nobody was allowed to get off the ship because the tenders couldn't operate safely in the roiling seas.

A few years later, I find myself onboard the Caronia sailing around South America again with a stop in the Falkland Islands. I put in for all of the tours because crew was not allowed off the ship otherwise. The tender ride was uncommonly long and having crew as part of the mix of people was just too chaotic.

DRAT!

I didn't get a tour.

What to do? Can I be here a second time unable to see the place?

All I knew of it was from a vague newscast I remembered with a Royal Air Force plane flying around the islands during the British war defending the Falklands from Argentina. Some Argentines to this day will still say that the land is rightfully theirs. No names will be mentioned, but an equally desperate friend and fellow cast member entered the picture at this point. Both "A-listers" in the Shore Excursion Office, we had escorted every tour between the two of us and usually had our choice of whichever ones we wanted, a very lucky situation on this day. She went into the Shorex office begging and pleading her case. Her boyfriend was in the RAF and had a pal who was going to give us a private tour!

Our stakes doubled.

Magically, and most conveniently, my friend and I suddenly became "escorts" on non-existent tours, just added onto the sign-in list. Voila! My ticket to the Falklands! Oh, the finagling that goes on! If this was happening on the little Caronia, imagine the cover-ups occurring higher up. The Warren Commission, anyone?

Being a part of this international scandal was quite exciting and I don't have to feel so bad. Nobody was hurt and no wars began as a result of this handy paperwork.

We got off the ship with another one of our fellow "escorts" and immediately grabbed a cab to leave the area as soon as we could. The security officer lurked around and we couldn't risk our guilty souls being sniffed out by his fine-tuned instincts.

Why did Britain fight so hard for this territory?

Our tour was lovely, but sadly, mines still infest the land. November is the month to see thousands of penguins. It was February.

I reacquainted myself with my British pounds and accompanied by my fellow renegades, walked around Port Stanley spending them on the obligatory postcards and pub lunch. Sauntering back to the tenders, smug and stuffed, we noticed that a lot of crew had made it ashore. One particular officer onboard was known to go against the word of the captain and allow members of the staff to "accidentally" slip by. However, the teatime band and some of the waiters showed up late for their shifts because the tender line was too long for them to get back onto the ship on time. The captain flew into a rage.

An investigation was launched.

Uh oh.

My naughty triumvirate gathered and confirmed our "on a tour" tale. No joking or bragging was allowed in public. This was getting serious. Other cast members furious that so many had gotten off also moaned that my colleague and I "had tours" in the Falklands when we had them everywhere else, too. My guilt grew a weensy bit. We hustled over to the Shorex Office to make sure that our stories matched.

They did.

Ah. We ended up safe, never even questioned.

I HAD to get off the ship and I HAD to see the Falklands. I was tired of being "Mr. Goody Two-shoes".

Shh, don't tell!

Chapter 26:

STORMY WEATHER

Photographing lightning ON A MOVING SHIP is impossible. I learned this the hard way...

Inclement weather is inevitable at sea. Watching a rain cloud approach remains a unique sight. Miles and miles are visible on the horizon, including ominous clouds with their slanting, dark rain. Lightning storms are unforgettable, too, the ship engulfed in a huge vortex of sensational energy.

If only for a couple of days, bad weather is not so difficult to deal with. I know to keep my stomach full (ironically enough!) and take my seasick pills. When the rough seas continue for days and days, though, my body just wants to feel normal again. It gets tired of walking uphill all the time, and longs to lie horizontal and just sleep.

Cargo ships endure much worse weather than cruise liners. If the weather is that bad, the captain of a cruise ship will change course. The Royal Viking Sun had to divert around Cuba to escape Hurricane Mitch. We missed a port in Panama, but didn't hear any complaints.

The Caronia's front lounge proved to be the best vantage point during a storm, the waves rolling and crashing onto the bow. The stern had a great view, too, as the back of the ship was flat, offering glimpses of how extremely we bobbed up and down. I can't imagine what it would be like on a sailboat during one of these storms if we jostled around so much.

Waiters told of the thousands of dollars lost in crockery during bad weather. One night, my Italian chef friend cried upon seeing all of his beautiful cuisine splatter onto the galley floor. The shopkeepers tape down their merchandise and those in offices lock their drawers and secure the travel books with handy bungee cords.

In my room, picture frames and books, once neatly in place, constantly keel over. Everything ends up on the floor for a few days and I deal with the mess later. Some crewmembers have had to put their televisions on their floors for fear of waking up to loud destructive crashes and broken TV screens or worse, broken skulls. A friend living on a lower deck had to have his porthole cover screwed shut during storms. Otherwise, it was fun to look out and see the waves crash by, a reverse washing machine!

The poor comedians scheduled for the cruise usually performed their low-maintenance acts on rocky nights. Dancers couldn't dance and pianists couldn't sit at a massive instrument where with one false move, it became a mobile weapon capable of annihilating an entire first row of screaming innocents. But let's face reality here. On really bad nights, nobody sat in the ballroom watching ANY kind of show.

Those living in the bow of the ship had it the worst. They lived in nice big rooms, if oddly shaped, but constantly bounced all over and endured the bashing anchor. It had to be maddening.

During less extreme occasions, the show has to go on. Instead of heels, the ladies wear sneakers. Our dance captain modifies lifts to a lower level and changes double pirouettes into singles, just to keep everything nice and neat. Once, I went to kick my leg, but wasn't able to just because my balance was so thrown off right at the pivotal moment that I needed it. Another time, my cast was lined up taking our final bow. The ship pitched and all of us crossed our right legs over our left, in perfect unison, preventing what would have been a domino-like pile on the floor.

On the Royal Viking Sun, from Japan to Hawaii, we encountered such bad seas that the ship lost a swinging gate out on its back deck and one of the thick metal railings was violently twisted out of shape. How does water DO that?

We spent a whole extra day wobbling at sea and losing time, arriving at Honolulu in the middle of the night. I have never seen so many crewmembers gleefully disembark, despite the hour, after eight tough days at sea.

But the deck chair mattresses dry out, the crockery gets replaced at the next major port, and all of the fallen books go back up onto their shelves. The ocean is calm again and vacation continues. That is life at sea.

Chapter 27:

THE TABLES ARE TURNED FOR A DAY

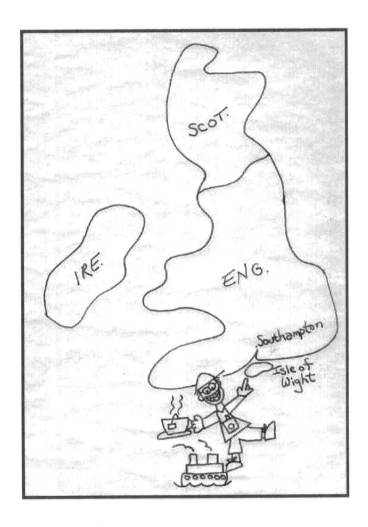

Some passengers became good friends. Such was the case with my British friend, Dawn. She was a gutsy gal, telling passengers to be quiet if talking too loud during the morning lectures we'd attend together. We'd also compare tours we were doing to see if I'd be her escort on any of them.

During the summer, Dawn invited me to the Isle of Wight. She lived on the island, a high-speed ferry ride away from Southampton where my ship docked. I would have my own personal tour guide during a perfect little side trip!

Dawn chauffeured me all over the charming hilly island, stopping at scenic points such as the Brading Down overlook (how British!) and the quaint Adgestone Vineyard, indulging in a rich cream tea and enjoying the farm animals. The goats looked like they'd been electrocuted, funky chickens clucked about, and two whimsical ponies named Brownie and Garbo came up only to my hip.

Many Roman settlements are spread over all of mainland England and the Isle of Wight. Dawn is an archeologist and helped uncover a recently discovered Roman villa that was of special interest to me. I don't know why I love ruins, but perhaps it's just because we simply don't have them here in America. Imagining what occurred at these sites so long ago, brand new and full of life, is very intriguing.

A permanent structure now protects the villa and its mosaics from the harsh elements and we spent a fair amount of time mulling about and marveling that such vibrant color could be preserved after so many centuries. Undecorated mortar filled in for missing tiles, activating my mind to complete the ancient picture.

We passed the nymphaeum, a semi-circular stone-lined structure used for baptisms and healing ceremonies. A diagram demonstrated how an entire villa can become buried and forgotten over the years: the villa is abandoned, the wind blows tiles off of the roof, rain seeps in and weakens the structure, it collapses, bushes form, trees grow, their leaves bury the villa floor, nature takes over, and eventually, no remnants of a settlement remain. Happening over the course of five hundred years or so, a farmer then comes along to serendipitously discover a foundation and the archeologists move in to excavate their new project!

Dawn's home was in the middle of some redecorating, but what a pleasure to be in an actual home for a change! From her bedroom window, she could look out on her perfect view of the ocean and see my ship sail out to veer starboard and head north for its next Baltic cruise.

Dawn wanted to take me into her yacht club before I left, but time ran out and no parking was to be found.

Huh.

I'd never been to a yacht club before.

Would I have made a fool of myself amongst her high-class friends? Did she HAVE high-class friends or were my imagination and insecurity at it again?

I ferried back over to Southampton from Cowes and arrived at my ship in time to check everybody's life jackets for boat drill. I was in the ballroom later doing sound check for my show that we had that night and parted the curtains to see our whereabouts. At that precise moment, Dawn's quaint little town drifted by, her house nestled in there somewhere, and I waved to my chum from afar as the Isle of Wight got smaller and smaller.

Chapter 28:

PLAYGROUND OF THE TSARS

The enormous Hermitage Museum rests on St. Petersburg's Neva River, a green and white wedding cake older than the United States. St. Isaac's Cathedral rises powerfully into the skyline, sheltering its magnificent malachite columns inside. The grandeur of this city is melancholy, long past its prime. When the city celebrated its tercentennial much was done to refurbish the landmarks and make St. Pete's more tourist-friendly, but grime still coats this treasure.

Only after six overnight visits to St. Petersburg did I feel like I had seen and experienced most of the sites available. One day alone must be set aside for a trip to Moscow. While the former Winter Palace of the tsars, the aforementioned Hermitage, can be rushed through in a morning, a whole day should be allotted there, as well. And two separate day trips are necessary in order to explore just a pair of the former tsars' country residences: Peterhof and Catherine's Palace.

Though extensive grounds surround the palaces, those at Peterhof are better tended with numerous fountains and terraces that aim to rival Versailles. When I visited Catherine's Palace, a blue and gold-domed fantasy, its famous Amber Room had recently reopened. My group was one tiny fraction of the anxious horde waiting at the entrance gates to experience this internationally acclaimed sensation. We were not disappointed. Imagine the walls of a decent-sized room decorated entirely with thousands of amber pieces!

But back to the actual city of St. Petersburg…

The cruise to the Baltic was always popular and sold out quickly. During my first call to St. Petersburg, we docked right in the city, a short walk from the Hermitage. We had to go through customs in order to get off of the ship and carry our passports with us at all times. This is not normal. On subsequent visits, as a result of silting and a more crowded river due to the city's big anniversary, ships docked much further away, making it very difficult to get into the city without escorting a tour. Passengers had to either sign up for tours or remain onboard. As a result, there would be people attending up to three shore excursions a day! They dropped into their beds at night, only to attack two more tours before sailing away on day number two.

Strolling by the powerful statue of Peter the Great himself, a bunch of friends and I stumbled upon a wedding party being serenaded by a brass street band. The bride's veil blew delicately in the wind as she struggled to neaten up for her photographer. We continued down the Nevsky Prospekt, the city's main thoroughfare, and I looked at a long structure to my right, a curvaceous and regal theater. Suddenly, turning left, the most improbable building came into sight, a colorful circus of a cathedral! The Church of the Spilled Blood, very similar to St. Basil's Cathedral in Moscow, dazzles with color and geometric whimsy. Its turquoise and chartreuse domes amongst spiraling spikes transform anyone away to fantasyland.

And to go inside! The visual feast continued with an overwhelming array of gold leaf mosaics, depicting religious stories from the Russian Orthodox Church. During every visit to St. Petersburg, I stopped by this cathedral and allowed its beauty to wash over me again. Several painters planted themselves along a nearby canal, capturing its complex shapes with their oils or watercolors. A plethora of vendors in the area sold the ubiquitous nesting dolls, amber jewelry, and detailed lacquer boxes, too.

A friend and I dared to take a local bus once. I had no idea how this particular system worked for not only were any announcements intelligible to me, but with the different Russian lettering, no place names could be recognized. My travel buddy had a bit of an idea where he was, so I just played "dummy" for the day and followed along.

Deteriorating apartment buildings blurred by and we soared over many of the city's canals, occasionally occupied by flat tour boats. Suddenly, we jumped out, my friend recognizing some random neighborhood. The bus deserted us in its putrid diesel cloud and we descended below street level to enter an authentic Russian restaurant, so much so that we were the only ones not speaking the language. An English menu wasn't even available, but one appeared with ever-handy pictures.

Always prepared, my friend pulled out his basic Russian phrase book and did an admirable job ordering for us, one of those amazing people who knows a little bit of a lot of languages. He ordered borsht and I dined on beef Stroganoff served with rice. How could I not?

The ballet is a must and I attended twice. The first time, I spent a mere thirteen dollars to sit in a marvelous booth for "Swan Lake". I had triumphantly found the theater where the show was, passing a couple guys playing chess (perfect!), and learned somehow that empty seats were still available. However, although street vendors took them, American dollars were not accepted at the box office. I had to run around from one dingy bank to another, showing my passport and practically donating a limb and firstborn kid before I could grab onto some rubles.

Interestingly, videotaping was NOT prohibited during the show and I observed a shaggy headed chorus dancer planning his evening out during the prima ballerina's solo. He didn't even try to mask his mouth! Despite this odd distraction, I was thrilled to see the prima ballerina perform in her program the climactic thirty-two fouette turns with spectacular strength and grace.

The second time I went to the ballet was with a crew tour. Paying for our tickets on the ship, we bussed into town for a very disappointing "Swan Lake". Chorus dancers phoned in their performances and the male lead lacked power. The prima ballerina cut those famous turns we had anticipated.

This was a dramatic case of being better off finding something on my own.

Set on the other side of the Neva River, the star-shaped Peter and Paul Fortress is not as easy to get to on foot as other sites, but still worth a visit. It lies inside a grassy park where I saw a man attempting to fly a kite with his enthusiastic little boy. The cathedral within the grounds contains the graves of the exhumed remains of the last royal family, a sobering monument to the bloody times that have managed to remain fascinating almost a century after their occurrence. Led into the former dark cells of the actual fortress, pictures of imprisoned convicts hung on the cold walls. One bore a striking resemblance to a bearded Brad Pitt!

I tried over and over to escort the tour to the Yusopov Palace, but it never worked out for me. Finally, with our last visit imminent, I went on the tour as a paying customer (weird for me not having to give my welcome speech or count people!)

One of many wealthy Russian dynasties, the Yusopovs lived in an elaborate home to rival the tsars'. I was interested in visiting this particular palace because the enigmatic Rasputin met his grisly death there and the tour included a creepy wax figure enactment of his final hours in the cellar. The Yusopovs had their own theater built into the palace and the library was to die for, a two-leveled room gorged with luminescent wooden shelves. We admired an elegant Moorish room, straight out of the Alhambra, and our guide turned our attention to a chandelier that was actually made of papier-mâché! None of us would have ever known it.

St. Petersburg has become much more tourist friendly since my first visit. Currency exchange booths exist everywhere now and internet cafes have sprouted up like mushrooms after a good rain. The city begs for visiting, with at least three or four days necessary in order to begin doing it justice.

Chapter 29:

THE BIGGEST SKY I'VE EVER SEEN

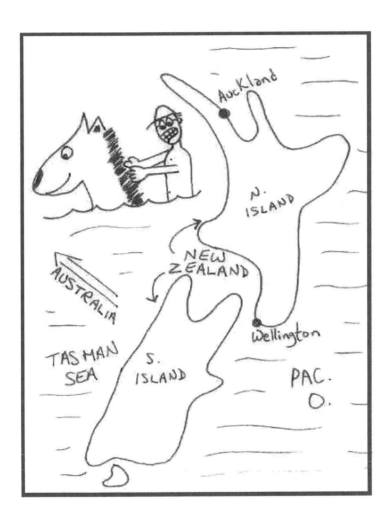

New Zealand.

A high school friend had lived there for a year. I visited before "The Lord Of The Rings" mania struck, but if I hadn't, my obsession with seeing all of the movies' locations would have negated my experiences that so defined this country for me.

My assistant cruise director had a sister who lived in New Zealand and when we docked in Wellington, he rented a car and invited three of us for a road trip to see her. Our hosts lived on a sprawling ranch, a refreshing change from the cosmopolitan city.

Our main activity for the day: horseback riding! My horse was a beauty named Goldie and together we traversed hill after rolling hill of prime sheep turf. This day was my proof that more sheep call New Zealand home than people. The gentle creatures grazed everywhere and I felt guilty disturbing their feeding time as they sauntered away from us distressfully bleating.

In minty air, we switched back and forth along steep hills, gradually climbing, and discovering new grassy nooks filled with, yes, more fluffy sheep! Wildflowers splashed color over the landscape and at one point we looked down onto a refreshing lake. The fields held giant-sized green marshmallows of wrapped silage. Starting back down, we'd hear sheep plaintively call out, and see them looking down at us in silhouette, their heads comically hanging over the hill from where we had just come.

Suddenly, we halted at a river. Our very rustic guide started to disrobe.

Hm…

This was an interesting development.

Wearing just his briefs, he climbed back onto his horse, Wilma, and crossed the river. Holding her mane in one hand with the reins in the other, he was bareback and told us that we could try it, too! The boys and I stripped down, our guide circling sweet Wilma back, and we plunged into the river with her one by one.

Enough of a shock to be on a horse while practically naked, it was even more so as my body gradually submerged into the cold river. Wilma must have loved it! She'd been working hard and swam like a champion, but her human cargo required more adjusting time. At one point the river deepened so much that I floated off of her back, my body still in complete shock, struggling to hold onto her mane for dear frigid life.

The highlight of the experience was to see my friend Brent's expression when he dropped his pants and realized that he was wearing smiley face boxer shorts! Four pale guys in their skivvies didn't quite cut the same figure as our rugged, bearded, and very tan Kiwi guide, but I think he appreciated our enthusiasm to just go for it.

On the way back to the ranch, we found the most amazing ice cream. For the equivalent of four American dollars, we ate six double-scooped cones, very sweet and fatty, just what we craved after our long day out as half-naked cowboys.

Our hosts' ranch sprawled out before us, wide open to settle down and be present with. The sun glorified all of our surroundings as it set behind the strong mountains and long blades of grass nestled us as we indulged in Mother Nature before heading back to help prepare dinner.

The ranch house was built as the money became available to do so. Plastic covered some of the walls and the rudimentary bathroom had no running water. My previous camping skills came in handy as I chopped colorful vegetables by candlelight!

We sat around the campfire gnawing on barbequed steaks and sausages along with bread made from whole kernels of corn. The company was fantastic and our day could not have been better. We ventured out into the pitch dark one last time.

Every single star shone that night, the biggest, clearest sky that I had ever seen. The Milky Way a still pond, the Southern Cross (and its "fake"!) was shown to me. We even counted many satellites! I had no idea that that many could be seen, blasting around with their precise mechanical jobs.

Alas, time to depart from our secluded paradise. We expressed our gratitude and were told by our hostess that she was proud to have met us. What a nice thing to say to somebody! Was that a Kiwi thing, to express such pride? Our hosts had big hearts and I very much respected their love of the land.

The boys and I reluctantly climbed back into our rental. We had had such a memorable night of bonding. Dark and curvy roads led us back towards brightly lit Wellington. The stars gradually disappeared, our big sky turning lighter and lighter.

Chapter 30:

TRUE LOVE

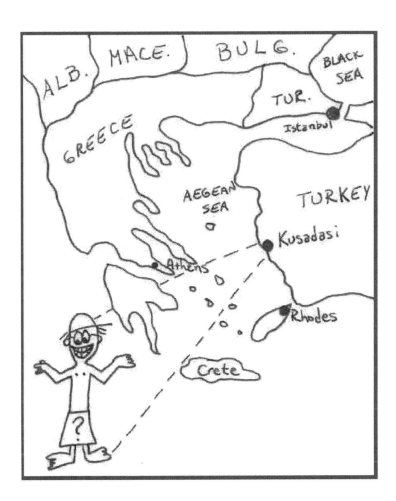

Instant friends!

Can somebody explain this phenomenon? I experienced an unmistakable connection to my fellow co-worker, Suzannah, when I first met her in the Miami airport. She understood my humor and became my fellow "scholar of life".

Caught somersaulting across a four lane highway during rehearsals while humming the "Mission Impossible" theme and "escaping" our imaginary enemies, others in the cast soon learned to just leave us in our own strange world.

Being together onstage proved dangerous. If she looked at me the wrong way, my professional demeanor shattered. She was my cool little sister, but we had to sing Cole Porter's song "True Love" to one another.

Singing a love song to your sister?

We could not keep straight faces during rehearsals while singing that dreaded tune. This hang-up tortured me and was completely out of my control. We tried one day to sing as country stars, Cockney characters, ANYTHING to get the madness out of our systems. The cast would gather in front of us to watch the imminent crumble. We temporarily conquered the hysteria once our producer came in to see our progress, but the agony of performing the song did not end that day.

Oh, no.

Our Cole Porter revue included a tap number before our duet together. One night, the delicate notes of the song's introduction starting, I grabbed Suzannah's hand and walked lovingly out onto the carpet surrounding the ballroom floor. Right as I opened my mouth to sing this lovely ditty into her eyes, she stepped upon the hardwood and we could both hear the mood killing metallic "tap, tap" of her unchanged, forgotten shoes…

We were in the middle of a SHOW, five hundred passengers watching us! I was PAID to remain professional, yet this was my silly buddy! O holy Muse of Calm, what to do?

Her eyes widened as I squeezed mine shut. Tears formed, hanging precariously from my lids. I took a deep breath, uttered a desperate prayer, and thought of dead puppies as I croaked out the first few notes. I bit my tongue while she sang, surely producing blood, and looked at her forehead during the whole tune. Sweat gushed out of my pores and we somehow survived the horrific trial.

A few weeks later, I forgot to change MY tap shoes.

From then on, our permanent ritual included checking the bottoms of our feet before entering for that cursed number.

Frances Mayes, author of <u>Bella Tuscany</u> and <u>Under the Tuscan Sun</u>, lectured on one of our cruises. Suzannah and I had read both books, attended all of her lectures (taking NOTES, that's how geeky we were!), and even found ourselves STALKING her in ports! She fascinated us, a real-life writer, so easily accessible for a few weeks. I dreaded the day when I'd read Ms. Mayes' next bestseller describing two cheesy dancers who followed her around in Rhodes, Greece and took every photo that she did, figuring, "If Frances likes this view, then it MUST be good."Luckily, when her next book came out, we were spared.

Our Turkish bath experience in Kusadasi went anything but smoothly. Suzannah and I were two Westerners who simply had no clue what to do! Not many people were there for us to "copy", either, and quite awkwardly, Suzannah was the only girl at the place.

Fees paid up, we entered the simple reception area with no signs visible or other doors obvious. Where did we change? The tired woman at the window impatiently pointed toward some tiny curtained anterooms and we each went in, hoping that this wasn't the secret exit for loser people who look like fools. We both came out wearing sarongs, but I was naked under mine. Suzannah wore her suit. Didn't we HAVE to get naked at the Turkish BATH?

We stood around for a bit longer, thinking that perhaps somebody would come out and elucidate us.

Nope.

The helpful window woman was humbly consulted again. Completely disgusted with us by now, she dismissively pointed in the direction of the steam room, which proved to be quite ineffective. Pints of toxins left our bodies, but our stress levels built up again upon realizing that we didn't know how long to stay in THIS room.

WHAT WAS GOING ON HERE?

Finally, a large Turkish man came in to retrieve us and we found ourselves in an expansive room with marble stalls where we were doused down with powerful hoses, much like smelly zoo animals. Stumbling up onto giant marble tables, we received our loofah treatments. My Large Turkish Man worked wordlessly. He deftly folded my sarong in such a way that 97% of my body was exposed. I was finally enjoying this.

But then, Large Turkish Man forcefully flipped me over and just about pulled off my bits when he roughly yanked up my sarong to cover my crack (God forbid it show at this point!) After this, I was literally slid over to the next Large Turkish Man down the assembly line and given a delicious back pounding and rub down with soap.

For eight dollars more, we could've gotten oiled up, but we had had more than enough by this point, our lovely introduction to the Turkish bath. Our respective men wrapped our heads Arab-style and we hysterically crawled away to change.

In Istanbul, the only city that spans two continents (!), Suzannah and I quickly bounded off the ship, running like kids towards a candy shop with cameras dangling off our necks. Hagia Sophia, composed of uneven floors and crumbling mosaics of Christ, and the Blue Mosque, decorated with dizzying tiles and carpeting, beckoned.

Topkapi Palace's harem stunned us with its flamboyant architecture.

Entire rooms contained tortoise shell and mother-of-pearl inlaid patterns, marble carved above-relief, or colorful stained glass windows depicting delicate flowers. The sultan's throne dripped with emeralds!

The pungent spice market delighted our senses. Piles of color! I grabbed a street gyro for lunch and a beverage called "Uludag" somewhere within our day, but then suddenly, embarkation duties loomed. Racing back to the ship, grilled corn in each hand, we had about five minutes to shower, change, and report to our respective posts. While greeting the new passengers, we learned that the ship was to sail late! There was time to go back out and do MORE!! How many times do you find yourself in Istanbul, Turkey? Would we ever come back? Suzannah, my fellow adventurer, was always game to cram into port time as much as humanly possible.

Returning to the market area, we watched the carpet men hauling their cumbersome rolled goods from warehouse to store. What a surreal sight to see so many plastic wrapped, colorful caterpillars slowly making their way up stairs and about town! I purchased walnut-stuffed apricots at another market and we sipped tea out of communal cups. At first I was a tad freaked out by the sharing, (was there really such a thing as "cooties"?) but our vendor casually wiped out the cups and in the end I figured, "when in Rome..."

Suzannah and I sat at a local restaurant where I discovered how delicious yogurt and tomato sauce are with chicken. We had completely eaten our way through Istanbul.

A murky sky settled in, our whirlwind day drawing to an end. Eerie prayer calls droned from the city's many minarets and a full bag of Turkish Delight was mine to enjoy at sea. The sun lowered and a chill came into the thick air. There was still enough light, however, for me to sneak a tiny bit more video footage of Frances Mayes and her husband, being tourists just like me and my pal, Suzannah.

The wicked witch's monkeys surround her in the dark forest, vomiting otherworldly sounds…

Bali is by far my favorite port in Indonesia. It was also my first and the one that most strongly impressed itself into my mind.

Anchored in Padang Bay, an innumerable amount of locals in their long canoe-like boats with skiffs on either side greeted us. The juxtaposition of our luxurious ship and these less-fortunate people approaching it for money and pillow chocolates that the passengers readily threw to them was hard to believe. They dove into the water after the tossed goods and I felt guilty, realizing that circus animals are watched and enjoyed for "doing tricks", too.

Once ashore, villagers selling their wares desperately inundated us. The most aggressive sellers I have ever encountered, what they offered was beautiful: hand crafted baskets, colorful and inexpensive sarongs, and many wooden carvings.

Two things immediately struck me as we set off with our driver, Ketat (meaning "fourth born"): terraced rice paddies not only sparkled with the most brilliant green against the deeper hues of the background jungle vegetation, but the land was cut into curvaceous, appealing contours. Huge marble sculptures decorated the intersections of Bali's major roads.

A Hindi temple called Besakih was in the midst of a festival that only occurred once a decade! How lucky to catch this! Before we entered, all of our legs had to be covered, men included. Our newly purchased sarongs suddenly became practical. The devout filled the temple and offered up delicious bowls of fruit and flowers. It was strange to us that these beautiful foods would just lie there for the gods and "go to waste" on the altars, but this was their custom.

Bali is a very artistic island, each village specializing in a different craft or skill. We passed through the silver and goldsmith villages, the umbrella village, the colorful incense village, the weaving, furniture-making and stone carvers' villages, and most impressive of them all, the woodcarving village. Exquisitely handcrafted, these carvings were some of the best I have seen in the world. Detailed dragons, each one of their numerous curvy scales painstakingly presented, tempted me into a purchase. Life-sized Balinese dancers (that we would later see perform) seemed alive, each dazzling jewel and delicate flower in their hats, each detail of their complicated clothing and serene faces depicted. Carved fishing nets and baskets from the native wood sat on display, too.

Donning our sarongs again, twenty cents each allowed us to enter the claustrophobic caves of Goa Gajah full of aromatic sandalwood offerings. There, amongst manicured paths to a waterfall, I captured two smiling kids on film, handing them some coins in return.

From here we made the "required" stop in Bali: the monkey forest at Sianyar. The macaques wandered throughout us visitors looking for one thing only—food. Anyone thinking that a banana could be hidden from these guys was just wrong. A few unfortunate children had some teeth flashed at them from an angry monkey, resulting in immediate tears and panicked running back to mom and dad. One father thought he was preparing his toddling daughter for a cute picture of her feeding a monkey. Upon arming her with a harmless looking banana, one of the critters barreled her over, grabbed the goods, and left the hysterical child rolling on the ground, growing up to wonder why she's mortally afraid of Curious George.

Macaques look very rat-like when wet, playing in their little swimming hole. For a fleeting moment, I missed the New York City subway system.

In the jungle area of this park, I found an ancient vine-covered temple reminiscent of the opening scene in "Raiders of the Lost Ark". Monkeys here and there added to its mystique. All of a sudden, I heard a distant simian scream of alarm and was freaked out to discover that every single monkey in the park was running toward me. I was frozen in my place, sinking into the mossy ground. I happened to be at the end of a bridge with dragon sculptures supporting its span and the monkeys jumped off of the stone railings and stormed right by me on either side, thankfully ignoring my presence.

I did not want to leave Bali. So much more of the island remained to be explored. I hadn't even focused on its bird life! Someday I'll return to this magical place with much anticipation.

Chapter 32

KING OF THE MOUNTAIN

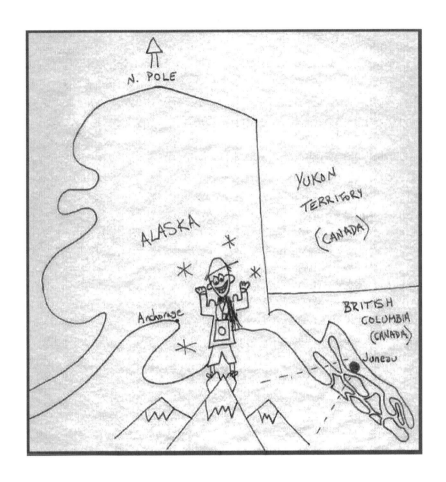

Alaska is big.

I will say this again.

ALASKA IS BIG!!

Most ships, ours included, cruise along the Southeast Passage. We hiked in all of our ports and took side trips to fly over glaciers or visit sled dogs. We saw what felt like a great deal of Alaska, yet looking at a map, I realized that 99.96% more of it was available!

An adventurous group of hikers and I planned our next outing: the great Mount Juneau towering over Alaska's capital city. Supplied with trail mix and donning sturdy boots, our group of ten anticipated a rugged day of exploration and natural beauty. Other hikes already completed that summer came to mind. How would this one compare?

Seward offered a hike deep into "Jurassic Park"-like forest area, concluding with a waterfall as reward for the trek. The path's isolation was such that I felt like one of the first humans ever to enjoy its pleasures. This was an easy day with relatively flat surfaces, yet we ran into nobody else on the trail.

Another hike in Seward scaled Mt. Marathon, overlooking the city. Four hours to climb this difficult peak, challenging because most of the path was loose gravel, made for a long day. How wimpy did we feel to learn later that every year, athletes race and conquer its heights in less than an hour! Some climbed it once per day!! This hike felt dangerous, sliding uncontrollably for most of the descent and having to jump down a treacherous rock face at one point in order to clear the previous level.

My "Mt. Juneau Ten" set out into the crispy day with overcast skies, our mood jovial and friendly. Soon left behind was the last bit of residential area. A raging river, for those who dared venture that close, provided icy refreshment. Thick vegetation lined our path and I marveled at how much one of the rivulets had thawed since my last hike I had taken there. Abandoned sawmills littered the landscape and offered the eye a change from the endless pine trees, sentinels of the forest. And although the sounds of nature are the best music, we purposely kept our chatter up, hoping to prevent an encounter with a grumpy grizzly bear.

Gradually we started to climb. Thigh muscles flexed and our boots performed brilliantly, clinging onto muddy rocks. Exhilaration built. Our end result was unknown. What would be discovered along the way?

The path eventually narrowed and we continued single-file. Tree roots had to be grappled at points, in order to safely ascend. How awesome was this? I felt secure, my boots and jeans richly mud-splattered, and I was WORKING!

Before long, the tree line laid below us, underneath the clouds! Someone requested another rest stop and we layered up with our anticipated sweatshirts. Our mountain could've served as one of the backdrops for the movie "Braveheart". Except for our cameras, we had transformed into Scottish warriors, stomping our way to the next battleground, traveling on grassy inclines and hiding behind enormous glacial boulders.

Our fantastic vantage point required utmost patience. Clouds obscured the view and the wind worked on its own time to blow the opaque moisture out of our sight. But suddenly, three thousand feet up, through a small hole in the sky, the remarkable view of our tiny toy ship and three others docked in the harbor appeared! We had arrived here by our own strength, well worth tomorrow's inevitable soreness.

A critical point was reached. After this break ended and the sky closed in again, everyone felt that they had had enough and turned back. I could not. I wanted to say that I had climbed the full three thousand, four hundred and fifty-six feet of Mt. Juneau. So I trekked on solo, leaving foot after foot below and behind, slowly remembering how deceiving climbing can be. I could see the top, just a few feet away, but arriving to where the "top" was, the land had only formed a bit of a plateau. My journey was far from over. Climb. Plateau. Repeat.

The clouds thickened, the air cooled even more, and the path became more difficult to follow within the rugged landscape. Two other adventurers snuck in and became my silent companions and I felt safer, knowing that other souls shared this experience near the summit with me.

Then, quite anti-climatically, we peaked. Trumpets did not announce us and the red carpets were gone for cleaning that day. Not even a wooden signpost present to verify our triumph, we simply had no higher to go. I was finally King of the Mountain. One of my fellow hikers was kind enough to take my photo for me as proof and then I let him be King, reciprocating the favor.

We did it.

Climbing back down Mt. Juneau took a third of the time and I happily met my pals at our favorite eatery, deserving every pizza slice that I soon inhaled. I never looked at the mountain the same way again. It no longer served as just a background. I thought of it more as a friend.

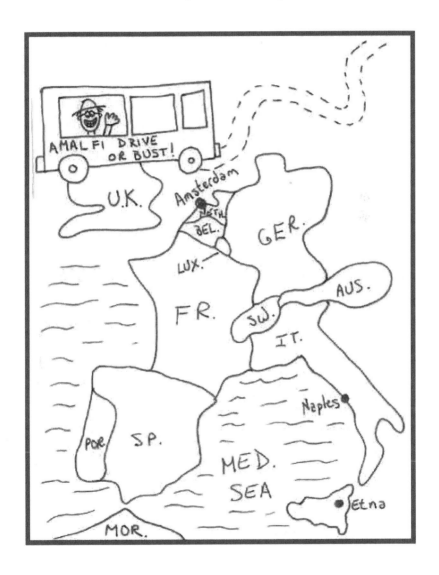

Her cell phone rang. With impeccable Queen's English, my guide
answered it, paused, and replied, "On the top of Mt. Etna"...

Every tour bus dispatched for a shore excursion has a guide onboard. They are locals and always very knowledgeable. I met several and they could be CHARACTERS!

On the first Mt. Etna tour that I escorted, our excellent guide was the British equivalent of Cyndi Lauper. Colorful and quite dramatic, she performed the local facts and lore. On the tour again two years later, interesting enough to repeat because the volcano had erupted since my last trip, I was able to see where the lava flow had been diverted and how the road up to the restaurant we lunched at was considerably higher due to the excess effluvia. More interestingly, my guide reminded me so much of "Cyndi" that I just had to ask if she knew her. "Oh, yes", she remarked. "You must mean my daughter." The mother had us all in stitches many times, not only in the ancient Greek/Roman theater at Taormina where she recreated multiple actors, but also in casually answering her cell phone with such aplomb on the top of an active volcano!

Then there was Amsterdam Ellen. I fell in love with her instantly. She made me guess right away where she was from (Indonesia) and kept the fact that she had just had her eyes done no secret. We managed a visit to the world-famous Rijkmuseum, closing for a years-long multi-million dollar renovation the next day! I hated to say good-bye to this warm woman, but was thrilled later on when I was invited out to dinner with the Shore Excursion staff and Ellen herself as our hostess!

She selected a hard-to-find Indonesian restaurant for us and even called ahead to order special food. Times like that reminded me to sit back and bathe in gratitude for a job where I got paid as an entertainer to sail all over the world and meet such hospitable people.

Unique and tasty, the food delighted us. However, I approached the mutton course skeptically. I am not one for most meat besides beef and chicken, but Ellen insisted.

It was CANDY! I never had better lamb in my life and I probably won't ever again. We all dove into the stuff as if it was ambrosia. This woman knew what she was doing and we laughed a lot that night, learning more about her interesting life and family.

Six months later, in Amsterdam again, I was lucky enough to feast on a canal dinner cruise guided by none other than fantastic Ellen. She looked great and we laughed together some more. It amazes me how quickly I can feel like I know somebody in such a disparate part of the world.

Last, but certainly not least, I met Pat on my Amalfi Drive tour from Naples, Italy. She wore a large yellow sundress and sandals. This woman, like my two Mt. Etna gals, was also a British ex-patriot. What is it with British women marrying Italian men and becoming tour guides?

Pat made me laugh the whole day with her dry sense of humor. It was the perfect day for this spectacular tour. The Mediterranean sparkled, clouds had taken the day off, and every impossible turn along the famous Amalfi Drive was both death defying and outrageous with surreal vistas.

I had introduced myself to Pat, as I always did with my guides, and gave my spiel over the bus microphone to everyone else: "Hi, my name is Mike. I'm one of the production show singer/dancers and I will be your escort today. If you have any problems, let me know and I will do what I can to assist you", etc.

Pat took over on the mike and spoke of all the oranges and huge lemons that we would see that day (she wasn't lying) and everything was proceeding smoothly. Our bus didn't careen into the Med once. Overlooking Positano during a photo stop, Pat approached me and said, "It's beautiful, huh, Mark?"

OK.

I'm NOT Mark, but that's fine. "Mark" is close enough to "Mike" and she's hilarious, so who cares?

Essing through the ribbon of a road, stunned that the driver never broke a window along the narrow and old passages, I literally sat at the level of the terra cotta roof tiles we snailed by. We applauded for our driver Giuseppe many times that day.

Accessible only by climbing a bunch of steps, I was down at the bottom of the cathedral in Amalfi letting all of the passengers ask Pat their questions before scuttling off to shop and explore. Alone with Pat, we stood right by a little shop that sold the local liqueur: limoncello. She turned to me and asked, "Have you tried this yet, Alan?" (Alan now!) "You really must. It's natural Viagra". Pat emitted a deep phlegmy smokers' laugh.

Quite yummy, yes, I believe that Pat had already had enough limoncello for the day. I was on name number two, but she was kind enough to procure a free sample of alcohol for me, so the mouth stayed zipped once again.

Plus, I was DYING to hear who else I'd be by the time we parted.

The last leg of our journey commenced and at one point, our driver rolled the bus' side mirror in to avoid its being crushed against the already damaged plaster walls of the whitewashed homes we passed. Crowded Sorrento became our last stop and we took the highway "home".

What a magnificent day!

Everyone safely left the bus and I thanked Pat, telling her how memorable (HA!) this tour had been. She gave me a great big bear hug and said to me, "My pleasure! I hope to see you again sometime, Chris!"

Chapter 34:

IN THE FOOTSTEPS OF GRANDMA

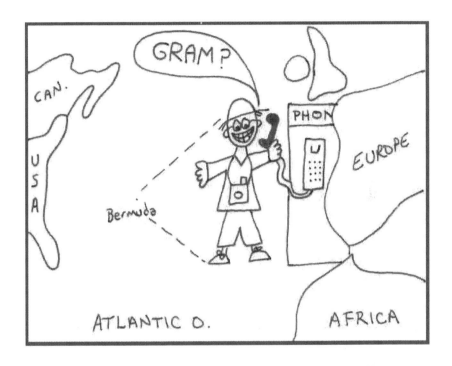

The year is 1934, and Eleanor has just found out that she will be spending her Easter season in Bermuda. What an opportunity! Her employer at the hotel in Lake Placid, NY has connections with the Atlantic island and permits some of his girls to go over for the busy two months. The waitress' boat trip will be paid for; they will make a minimal wage, and keep all of their tips. Eleanor is twenty years old.

She takes the train to New York City and catches her ferry to Bermuda. Unfortunately, Eleanor does not take to the sea very well, and the journey is rather unpleasant. But once on the island, all of that is forgotten. She will be working at the beautiful Princess Hotel, staying in a room where poinsettias grow wild right outside her window! And it's not even Christmas!

On her day off, Eleanor takes a horse and carriage around the island with some of her girlfriends. They enjoy seeing the lilies growing abundantly all over the land and finish their ride at Elbow Beach, popular for its pink sand, for some much-deserved relaxation in the sun...

Over sixty years later, Eleanor's grandson has called to inform her that once again, he has a contract to perform on the Cunard Caronia. He'll be sailing to many exotic ports.

"Didn't you work in Bermuda once, Gram? My ship will be going there!"

Eleanor is delighted for her grandson and makes him promise that he will shoot lots of video footage and tell her all about the current state of the island.

Once in Bermuda, Mike manages to see most of it during his limited eight-hour visit, bussing to St. George's via Elbow Beach. There is no time to get off of his bus, though, and see if the sand is really pink. Mike has one more special task to fulfill.

He stops in Hamilton to find the Princess Hotel. During the bus ride, he was alarmed to discover that TWO Princess Hotels operate now in Bermuda, but the one in Hamilton is much older, the only one existent in 1934. Making his way inside the lobby through a beautiful arched entryway, Mike activates his video camera and takes extensive footage of the grounds and public space of the hotel. Fountains pour out of the walls; there is a koi pond in the back of the establishment. He has had to wait until the afternoon to do all of this so that it won't be too early on the east coast to make his call. Mike finds a bank of public payphones and dials up his grandmother's number.

"Hey, Gram! Guess where I am? The lobby of the Princess!"

The two had a lovely chat, as usual, and Eleanor got a kick out of hearing from Mike in Bermuda. Home for his next visit, he showed her his footage. He had filmed the restaurant and even went outside to the pool area and outlying buildings, thinking that they could've housed his Gram all those years ago.

But…

None of it looked familiar to Eleanor. Who knows how many renovations the place had undergone over so many years? Who knows if her specific work place was even still existent?

It didn't matter to Eleanor. She had her fond memories of Bermuda and was just happy that Mike was safely home once again. They sat down together in her cozy apartment and had some tea.

Chapter 35:

EXOTIC LAND OF WONDERS

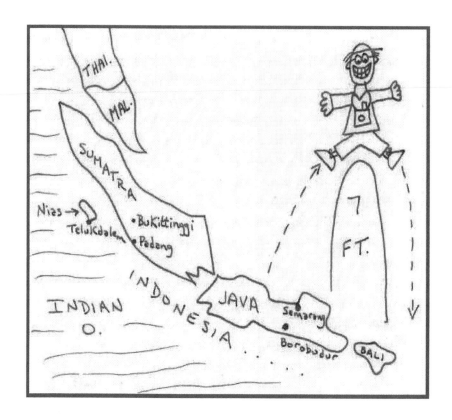

Bukittinggi, rambutans, and Karakatau, oh my!

Another advantage of my life at sea was the chance to better learn my geography. The subject got brushed over, at best, in my schooling. I didn't know a thing about Indonesia before arriving there for our two weeks. Comprised of islands numbering in the thousands, we visited only four of them!

Attending a lecture on the history and importance of Burobudur, a massive Buddhist structure, my interest was piqued. From our port, we hired a driver named Chito to drive us two hours on dusty, crowded roads. The green of the countryside provided harsh contrast to drab Semarang, Java.

Along the road, a man carrying an impossible load of little red fruits whizzed by. How bizarre! A huge bundle hung from the end of his stick and each individual piece of fruit looked like a miniature version of a red sea anemone--rambutans. Oh, yes! I had tried one somewhere before and enjoyed it. Chito pulled over so that I could buy some.

A generous bunch of the sweet fruits cost little. Very much like lichee nuts, the meat is harder to harvest from rambutans. Nonetheless, I enjoyed my fill and shared with everyone else who wasn't too chicken to try. The only disadvantage of this purchase was in looking down a few minutes later to discover that an army of ants had come out from hiding in the fruit to take over my sneaker.

Burobudur finally rose out of the forest, solid stone, and my fellow adventurers and I eagerly bypassed the opportunistic vendors in favor of starting our climb. The levels of the multi-layered structure each represent another step to Nirvana. We shared our hike with Muslim schoolgirls, fellow tourists as excited to meet us and take our pictures as we were of them. They giggled a lot around my very blond and model-looking pal, Brent.

Capping Burobudur, seventy-two Buddhas rest inside bell-like structures called stupas, and rubbing one of their feet brings good luck. Some of the decorative stones had been newly restored, some moldy and crumbling back to their source. All of them were carved lovingly with stories and rites from the religion, symbols that I could admire for their beauty, but appreciate only as an illiterate.

Tourists wriggled throughout this massive structure, enough room for us all, no matter the nationality. Even the rats sharing the floor with us in the restaurant we stopped at for lunch munched peacefully. The restaurant had no walls and the rodents' presence confirmed that whether we humans liked it or not, they had lived there first.

From Padang, Sumatra, we again hired a van and paid a visit to a little town called Bukittinggi. Eric was our driver that day for another long and hot trip, but with much greener vegetation. Temples rose colorfully out of the landscape, reminding us of the local religion. With architecture most elegant, the eaves of the roofs curved gently, culminating in perfect points.

Bukittinggi's visit had to be quick due to our distance away, but we did find a man painting idyllic country scenes on black velvet. Vibrant colors leapt from his easel and as if our imaginations hungered for more stimulation, he depicted the curvy temples with their wondrous inlaid wood designs set among waterfalls and sunsets with the most impossible clouds ever seen.

I will never forget this town with the funny name that we randomly decided to visit. Oddly enough, I later found out that one of my best friends from college married a man whose brother-in-law is from Bukittinggi! What are the odds of THAT?

Telukdalem on Nias Island was the most amazing stop we had in Indonesia. Everyone took the tour to the very rustic town of Bawomataluo. No modern busses with air-conditioning existed for this tour. Pick-up trucks outfitted with seats set up in back did the job, the Shore Excursion office warning everyone that a bumpy ride was to be expected. Shockingly, nobody complained!

Pristine countryside filled our eyes until we arrived at our town, at the top of an imposing set of stairs. Once level again, the locals greeted us, inviting us to wander about the town's single, wide street flanked by the unique bi-level structures of this community. With bottom levels wide open, sturdy log beams jutted out diagonally from the street level to support the upper floors. All of the homes sat uniformly, in a neat row on either side, some of the roofs containing an opening to allow the escape of wood smoke.

Many of the local people appeared afire in their ceremonial wardrobe of bright red, yellow, and black. The men carried shields and spears. The women wore long elegant dresses and gold bands on their heads. Everyone danced and moved in complex formations that would rival championship marching bands the world over. But the highlight of our day had not yet begun. We had come to see the jumpers.

Assembled in the street stood three solid and slightly tapering seven-foot structures that the most athletic men jumped very easily over. They hurled themselves over at such impossible angles and we went wild over the amazing feats. Even the locals not participating watched. This sport is unique to Indonesia, depicted on some of the country's currency.

After the excitement, a friend and I admired the houses again, and a local woman invited us into her home! I took a photo of her sweet children and climbed up her ladder to see the second story view. We felt honored by her kindness, paying a few rupiahs for her troubles.

Everything in Indonesia was exotic, even the commonplace, such as passing three men risking life and limb to load a water buffalo onto a flatbed truck! This was truly a different world.

One of the natural highlights of this country was to sail by Karakatau at night while active. The neon lava spurted out of its angry source like pressurized water continually for us. How could that be real? The rock flowed down the side of the volcano in multiple streams, burning everything in its path. The ship sailed away, but I kept out on deck for about two hours watching the spewing lava's fireworks display, shaking my head in disbelief.

With all that I experienced in Indonesia, the first thing I told my mother about the country is that we had to take malaria medication and watch out for pirates!

That was true, too.

Passengers filled out comment cards and rated every aspect of the ship after each cruise: stewards, waiters, cruise staff, ports visited (which never made sense to me—they chose the cruise, right?) The bane of our existence, ratings indicated whether our shows needed extra brush-up or whether somebody was just not quite on the right track yet with his or her performance. I disliked the idea of being rated, yet always anticipated seeing how we did. One of my cruise directors treated ratings as a game. He wanted all of those in his department to climb higher and higher: admirable, but maddening.

I had just gotten onboard with four other new cast members. Our current batch of shows had proven very difficult to learn, one having been taught in the impossible confines of the ship's hallways due to crunched time and unavailable rehearsal space. The company's main office required from us at least an 8 out of 10 for our shows, our producer wanted an 8.5, and our perfectionist cruise director wanted a 9.

Fine.

A tall order to fill, we felt as prepared as possible to open our show as a new ensemble. Our debut went over quite well. Of course, there will always be things to improve on for a new cast, but we had received nice comments when we greeted everyone after the show and felt proud to have just survived the ordeal of learning the shows so quickly.

The ratings tallied, the cruise director called me, the company manager, into his office. He looked down at his sheet and said, "9.06. Not good."

"NOT GOOD!?" ARE YOU NUTS? Boy, I really wanted to hit him. Now granted, the cast before had been getting much higher ratings, having performed for a year together, but we worked hard, sweat our butts off, managed the 9 he required, and still got, "9.06. Not good."

Our ratings steadily climbed from that cruise on.

The comment cards accompanying these ratings could be fun to read. Most passengers loved us. The ratings proved that. The following couple needed some winning over, though: "The show…was somewhat revolting….blah blah blah". Next they went on about how more material from the 1930s needed to be added to our 1960s rock revue. The comment then ended with, "I would recommend some polling of cruise guests before you invite this ***wild bunch of hoodlums*** on board again." They gave us a 2 (for the one show they bothered coming to) and more importantly, a hilarious quote for us to laugh at for the rest of our contract.

Then we had this one: "We thought the troupe were disappointing. Men, particularly, and most women like to see tall girls with long legs wearing short length skirts and high kicking. It started with Busby Berkley and still features in Chicago. They were dressed in trousers or nun's outfits, or even Little Bo-Peep dresses. I repeat, disappointing." Despite the perverted reasoning (uh, go to Vegas or Paris if you want to see showgirls!), they rated us with a 4 and a 5.

I was very lucky to have a job where the ratings basically took care of themselves. Our costumes knocked the audience's socks off. We merely wore them and did a few high kicks while singing some tunes.

A note: While this next chapter relays happy experiences with my favorite animal, the elephant, several years later I can no longer support the performances and riding of these terribly exploited animals.

Chapter 37:

MAHOUT MIKE

Thank you for letting me sit on your head. I will never forget that privilege…

Docking in Laem Shebang, Thailand, I escorted a tour to an elephant show that was quite fun, if circus-like (in other words, why bother doing that in Thailand when it could be done at home?), but I did pay a mere dollar to get my photo taken with a sweet Asian female. She wrapped her versatile trunk right around my torso, effortlessly lifted me, and got a banana for her reward.

My friend Brent had lived in Thailand for a summer. Imagine my surprise when this pale Midwestern dancer boy walked up to some unsuspecting locals and started speaking Thai! He impressed THEM!

Brent had loved "papaya bok bok" during his summer and suggested that I sample some, too. I found a vendor on the beach later, paid her another mere dollar and received an ample amount of the spicy and delicious coleslaw-like snack along with a Coke!

The next day, I arose early and caught a shuttle to what was the highlight of that contract for me: a long-awaited elephant safari at the Pattaya Elephant Village.

None of my friends could be roused, so this became an experience to savor on my own. Having collected elephants since I was a kid, I have always felt a deep affinity for and connection to the noble creatures. Ten to fifteen other people took the safari with me, but I was lucky in that, since I was traveling by myself and everyone else had partners, I got to ride my actual elephant alone!

After climbing to the loading platform, I carefully made my way onto the back end of my elephant, getting as comfortable as possible on the hard wooden seat strapped around its mini van-sized belly. An umbrella shaded me.

As the journey started, I tried to communicate with the mahout, the elephant's driver, but a complete language barrier separated us. He whispered encouraging commands to our pachyderm and I tried to establish HIS name, but I think he told me the elephant's instead!

Was he Patapet?

Hotep?

Kantan?

Green fields laden with water buffalo flanked us and at one point we crossed a river. Gliding quietly and smoothly over the terrain, the elephants were surprisingly graceful for such giants. I sat on my throne, a Siamese king, observing the way that my elephant's shoulders rhythmically raised and lowered as it walked along. The skin wrinkles would also come and go as it stepped forth--ironing out and crunching up. Midway, we had a little break, the elephants guided into shade. Most people climbed down off of their hard wooden seats, but I stayed up on mine "asking" Patapet/Hotep/Kantan with gestures if it would be all right for me to climb onto the elephant's head where he had been.

The mahout indicated that it WAS!

My very American white sneakers came off and I climbed out of my perch, settling happily onto the enormous skull of my transport. To be so intimate with an elephant and able to feel its skin with the bottom of my bare feet conjured up something primal in me. I admired the many course black hairs all over its head and the patches of pink skin that appeared throughout the animal's predominantly gray coloring.

And then its trunk snaked up to SNIFF me! My new friend was getting to know me and I reached down to touch the trunk. I sent my comrade so much love that day and was reluctant to relinquish my stately position.

Our ride ended soon after. I happened to find another worker there who spoke English and he told me that my elephant's name was indeed Boolam, meaning "old, goes forward".

I silently thanked Boolam for bringing me forward and not ditching me in the river.

Chapter 38

RENEGADES PART II: HONOLULU

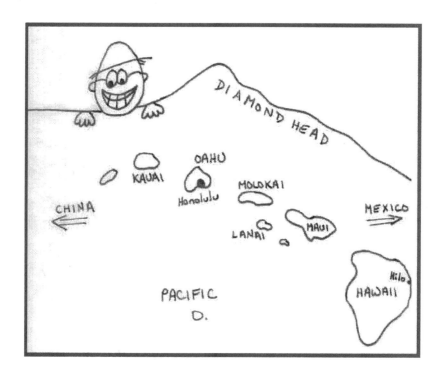

Playing "dumb tourists" can come in handy.

On the first cruise of my first ship, we sailed down the US coast, traversed the Panama Canal, and explored Mexico on our way to Hawaii! All seven of us in the cast split the library duty and on the day of one of my shifts, we docked in Hilo, Hawaii. In three hours, I rented a car, raced through Volcanoes National Park, returned the car, and got back to the ship.

In Oahu, I promised myself a more leisurely pace. A friend and I set off for Diamondhead on foot. This may have been great exercise, but a bit too leisurely. By the time we got to the park to visit the site, it was 6:30

and closed! Disappointed, but stubborn, we decided not to let this get in our way.

The "dumb tourists" idea kicked in. We simply walked around the chain that closed off the road to cars. "Oh, gee, Mr. Officer, we thought the park was only closed to VEHICLES." Our excuses all planned out, because Diamondhead housed a military base, we figured that we'd soon be discovered anyway.

Nope.

The path to the view overlooking Waikiki lay in front of us wide open. However, our light was fading fast. The sun had set behind the rim of the dormant volcano's crater and we suddenly came upon a tunnel! This was not good. Should we go in? Was it dangerous?

My partner had a brilliant idea. Literally. As proper "dumb tourists", we both had cameras. Both had flashes. The hilarity of this situation struck us as we started to photograph each other in order to light our way through! I have a whole roll of pictures cataloguing my sneaking amongst rough hewed rock walls like a blinded raccoon, alien-eyed, and wearing shorts with hiking boots. Posing with a knife in his mouth, my fellow hiker played "Bloodthirsty Headhunter Stalking Dinner". However, his prey was the sunset.

Emerging from the tunneled walkway, the fresh cool air felt much better than the staleness we'd been submerged in. The sunset complete, its aftermath was still spectacular. The hotel buildings downtown formed stark silhouettes against the vast pink sky, a rank of soldiers ready to battle. Some ominous looking clouds brought out the sky's color that much more. Tiny boats bobbed down in the harbor for the night. We had "conquered" Diamondhead!

No time to linger, we set off quickly before losing all light, creating more silly tunnel poses. But whoa! Right at the end of our trip, there in the distance, hairs on the back of our necks raised, a patrol car threatened! Would our escapades land us in the clinker after all? We found ourselves ducking, ironically enough, behind the stop sign posted to keep cars out of the park. Of course, still undiscovered, we had to take the time to capture THAT on film.

"Leisurely Walking Day" was over, and we bussed back into town where I met another friend for a luau. Every vendor that we encountered congratulated us as honeymooners, so we played along, making a lovely couple. Why not?

Escorting the tour to Diamondhead the next day, I took photos of the same scenes from the night before: morning and evening versions. Hand-held flashlights lit our way this time when entering the tunnel.

It just wasn't as much fun.

Chapter 39:

PETE THE PRINTER

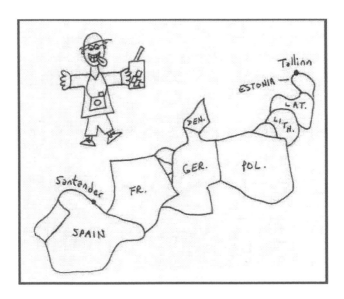

Like my fellow cast member Suzannah, my friend Pete and I made an instant connection. The printer onboard Caronia, Pete was from South Africa and I had just, coincidentally, taken a road trip right through the town where his parents lived! I harbor a deep affinity for Africa, Pete and I bonding immediately because of that.

Crewmembers always scratched their heads over our friendship. At first glance, we appeared to be very different people: I the theatrical entertainer type and he the beer guzzling, hang-out-with-the-guys-after-hours type. Because of my work, I was pretty clean cut, the boy-next-door, but I can be pretty tense at times. Pete was laid back with a shaggy 'do. But Africa connected us. He was amazed to meet an American stranger who had driven around treacherous foreign roads AT NIGHT that he knew like the back of his hand. We talked a lot about the places we had both visited and shared respect for their beauty. Pete was the only person on the ship who understood the primal feelings I had for Africa. I have always envied that Pete lives there and can go anywhere on the great continent much easier than I.

Pete was artistic, too, something that I learned after getting to know him better. A wonderful photographer, he generously opened himself up to me and shared his work. One of my most prized photographs is one that he took on the Etosha Pan in Namibia, a stop on one of my itineraries, as well.

If Pete and I made a plan, it usually got messed up. He'd have an emergency batch of menus to print, I'd have a last-minute duty to attend to, or our timing would just be off. But if I was just wandering down some lane in Tallinn, Estonia, or a crowded street in Santander, Spain, he'd be at the perfect outdoor café with a drink, I would join him, and we'd be set for the afternoon. Our accidental meetings ended up the ones where we'd have the best time.

Pete was somebody outside of my department who I could trust. We talked about situations that people got themselves into, but he always kept me in check, warning not to judge. He was helpful in reminding me that people are on their own journey for their own reasons. We have no say in what is THEIR right or THEIR wrong, a very valuable lesson from Pete.

His tiny hidden away office was convenient to my cabin and I could hop in and say hello at any given moment. I could rant and rave over who did/said what and he would just calmly listen, later putting all of the silliness back into perspective for me. He was my calming force on the ship, my objective voice of reason.

Someday I want to travel around Africa with Pete and see the land through his eyes. I want to rough it and camp out under the infinite African sky like he does. Our relationship will then come full circle. For now, though, I e-mail Pete the Printer, America to Africa, and hear about all of the latest that he has seen and photographed.

Chapter 40

A DAY OF MIRACLES

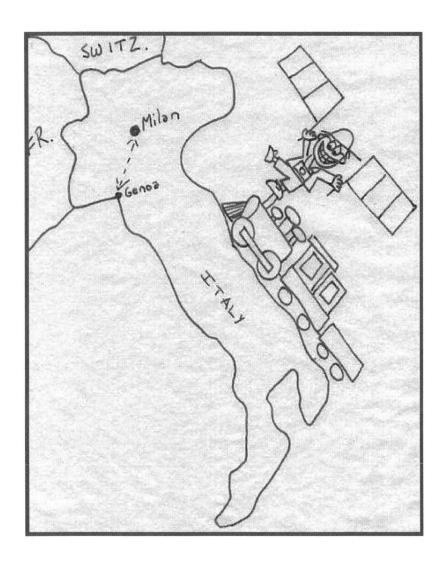

Whoever heard of Easter Monday?

On a solo train trip around Europe, I was in Milan for a few hours, trying to visit the Santa Maria della Grazie to view "Il Cenacolo" (da Vinci's "The Last Supper"), only to realize that I was there on Easter Monday!

Easter Monday? Huh?

The church was closed.

Later, after wondering how I'd fill my time during a second trip to Genoa by ship, I discovered that I could be very daring and attempt to see the painting again. My time was limited, the train schedule unpredictable, and I had no reservation to actually get into the church.

I quickly learned that there was a bit of the divine at work for me on this busy day.

I was prepared to race all the way across town to a railroad station but discovered one right by the ship! (MIRACLE #1!) Then I discovered I was running to the train with my bag open, money and ID flying everywhere! I luckily lost nothing. (MIRACLE #2) Then, the man at the station not only let me purchase my ticket with American dollars, but he kindly converted the rest of my money to lire, with no fee. (MIRACLE #3)

One and a half hours and a beautiful valley-filled ride later, I set off in Milan and immediately got lost. My memory from having been there eight years prior did not kick in and despite finding the main road and encountering lots of helpful folks, including some who had never heard of the Santa Maria della Grazie, I had to give in and buy a map. I found the church at 11:15 or so, quite late having arrived in town over an hour earlier, and the man checking people in initially told me, "it's impossible to enter". I told him I was alone and he said I could get in at 1:30. OK, I thought, but then remembered that my return train was at 2!

AGH!

I then figured I could take a later train since the station was so close to the ship. I went up to the ticket desk and the lady there told me that 1:30 was impossible and there was nothing available for earlier and she wasn't going to give me an inch! So I return to the gentler man outside and he suggested to me 3:30…impossible! But then he checked his clipboard for me yet again and said, "11:30".

What?

It was like an auction, but at least he was on my side. I stood there as he turned others away. (MIRACLE #4) I figured I had until 1 at the latest to get in, and at 11:30 my guy went to the ticket counter to act on my behalf. The adamant woman said, "No!", but he kindly told me to wait until 11:45. Maybe.

OK… so I'm waiting some more and another man shows up with an extra ticket!! (MIRACLE #5) I couldn't believe it! I have to say that I didn't think I'd get in, but with the effort to get there, the time and expense, I HAD TO GET IN and I consciously changed my mindset. The higher forces were on my side.

There was amazing security to get in. You go through the first door, it seals, you go through another. The light and humidity are regulated in the fresco's room. I was so excited I thought I'd cry! I couldn't read Leonardo's bio (in Italian) but that was fine. I entered the sacred space, first looking to my left, but then as I looked to my right, The Last Supper!

WOW! WOW!! I'd waited years and it was gorgeous, in such bad shape but still beautiful, a painting in ruin with cracked plaster, paint specks, and chips practically all that remain. I was able to videotape and that was a thrill, capturing specifics of paint. I was floored to see such detail on the table and the Apostles' feet with folds in the table cloth too. I chuckled to find the apostle, Matthew, that I had played in a production of "Jesus Christ Superstar" when we posed in a freeze to recreate this scene onstage. I was overwhelmed with awe.

My fifteen minute time slot was up and I exited to explore the gift shop, finding the comprehensive array of books on the subject including one that reproduced the whole thing in fold-out sections. I was very interested seeing detail so up close.

I thanked my extra ticket man again, the kind doorman, and had time left to explore more of Milan. I went in the Duomo with its billion grand spires and by the famous opera house, La Scala. Buying my return train ticket I remembered to validate it this time, something we don't have to think about in America, and had another nice ride back to Genoa, reading my "Last Supper" informational book.

This also happened to be the day I had to move out of my room, due to a new band leader arriving and I rushed to boat drill where a man almost (MIRACLE #6) clobbered me for telling him to keep his vest on. Life is so hard for a cruise ship passenger. After sound check, Patricia Neal, one of our Theater-At-Sea performers, asked me where the dining room was and I carelessly told her the wrong deck! Great. Luckily, she never held it against me.

MIRACLE #7.

Chapter 41

THE LONGEST RIVER IN THE WORLD?

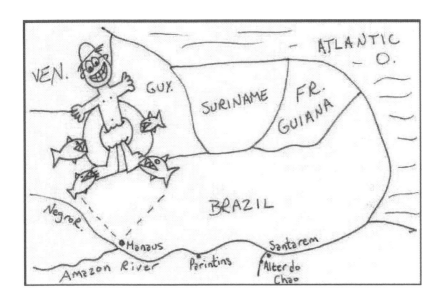

Everybody grows up learning that the Nile is the longest river in the world. But, some scientists have now said that the title must be turned over to the mighty Amazon of Brazil, as a new tributary has been discovered, ultimately beating out the African giant. Whichever river is longer holds no importance for me. All I know is that I was fortunate to work on a ship small enough to cruise down the Amazon River to Brazil's jungle city of Manaus.

My producer contacted me in the States wondering if I'd come back to the Caronia to finish the contract of my replacement. The job is not for everyone. Some feel claustrophobic on a ship. Some miss the conveniences of living on land too much. Initially hesitating to return to the same job after so little time away, I had no problem making up my mind once I heard the itinerary.

After meeting the ship and new cast in Florida, we did a few days in the Caribbean before sailing to the great South American continent. Fortunately, I knew most of the shows, but I did have to scramble and learn a fourth that had been added since my time there. How could I do this? The ballroom was constantly occupied and the gym jam-packed.

Enter my toilet.

Yes! My welcome back to the Caronia consisted of an overflowing toilet and flooded room. I was transferred to a passenger cabin that ended up being the perfect rehearsal space with lots of light and mirrors, albeit small.

During all of this readjusting, the water we sailed in gradually changed from a deep blue to murky brown. We had entered the mighty Amazon! Our days scorched and our nights cooled with heat lightning thrown in as a bonus. I would go up on deck as often as possible to inhale the earthy warm air and admire the trillions of stars. Sometimes it was hard to believe we were on a river, our passage was so wide. On other occasions, the ship sailed quite close to the riverbanks, very spooky in the dark. What lurked in the vine-filled tangle, looking back at me? A friend and I found many bug specimens one night, drawn to the numerous lights on the ship, of all different sizes and colors.

Huge logs floated by as if tiny twigs. We heard their hefty bulk make contact with our strong hull. Enormous masses of what looked like mangroves floated by, too, freshly torn from their underwater roots. Some harbored an egret, brilliantly framed by the rich green. The vegetation ample, I had trouble believing that areas existed where this lushness was being destroyed at a disturbing rate. The information didn't fit in with breathing all of nature's bounty at that moment.

All of a sudden, the clouds would sneak over and the sky would darken, opening up to replenish the river with tons more liquid. It landed with drops peaceful enough to enthrall me into sleep.

But who had time to sleep?

A tour from Santarem featured highlights on jungle harvests: manioc, the local staple, pressed to rid it of its fatal toxins; rubber, slowly dripping from diagonal tree notches; and Brazil nuts, growing in clusters within a coconut-like shell. One woman wore mosquito netting throughout the tour, yet had no qualms holding somebody's rat-like pet that looked as if it wanted her finger as its next meal. A tarantula web was pointed out to us.

In Alter do Chao, the "resort town" of the Amazon, we rented canoes and waded around the beach area that only hours before had been underwater. This town contained a very depressing museum stocked with artifacts from the innumerable indigenous people obliterated from the area when the Europeans invaded. Again, it was hard to fathom any kind of horror here when all else seemed so wondrous.

From Parintins we patronized the Boi Bumba show, a local troupe of hundreds that dressed with an orgy of feathers and danced to rousing music that had everybody on their feet. The show was performed specially for us and strong caipirinha flowed freely, a huge party in the middle of the jungle with everyone from the ship. Several locals came. I was particularly taken in with the young kids at the back who knew every word and move that the performers executed on stage. I watched them with fascination and knew exactly how they felt. A younger sister of the main performer onstage looked up to her elder sibling with pride. Some of the girls found out that I sang, requesting a few riffs from the latest boy band and they screamed for me, my little taste of American pop stardom.

The show featured beefy fire-eaters and my friend Pete placed himself right underneath the platform on stage where they stood in order to get an interesting photo. Little did he expect the shower of kerosene that they spit out after producing their thrilling breath. Pete reeked for the rest of the night.

Manaus, after nine days up the river, was a dirty and crowded city full of riff-raff, but our only chance to change money and check e-mail. From here, smaller boats could be hired that in five days transported the ultra-adventurous to Iquitos, Peru for eighteen dollars! I met an acquaintance who had made the trip and despite her abdominal woes, the tales of her explorations sold me on mentally adding the journey to my extensive "to do" list of travels.

The cruise featured lectures from a true-life explorer named Stanley Spielman. I was fascinated by his stories and wanted to convince him that I had to become his assistant! This man became friendly with indigenous tribes, still in the Stone Age by our standards, checking their eyes, and giving them second-hand eyeglasses. Imagine now a native man in the jungle, naked, and hunting with poisoned blow darts wearing glasses! Anachronistic, yes, but Stanley related how in some cases, the glasses were a matter of survival, the subjects unable to stalk their prey before his help. Very delicate work, Stanley must have been a patient and almost saintly man to have gained these people's trust.

From Manaus, I escorted a trip to a river resort, enjoying wooly and red-faced monkeys, hiking into the jungle, and swinging on a vine like Tarzan! There was also time to rest on an inviting hammock. We were given canoe rides amongst the dense tropical growth, passing pizza sized lily pads and vultures ominously drying out their ragged wings. Birds and other fauna filled the air with their calls. Coming back, we visited a local woman with passion fruit and cashew nut trees growing in her backyard. We also witnessed the famous "meeting of the waters" where the leaf-steeped blackness of one tributary (the aptly named Black River) meets the silty chocolate Amazon. The two distinct currents swirl around each other like an exotic candy until eventually blending miles down the river. Floating gas stations abounded.

I also participated in a late-night hunt for baby caimans, cousins to our alligators. We cruised along, the distant lights of the big city glowing on the horizon, an elegant palm tree in silhouette, and the spotlight shone on two beady red eyes. The drivers pulled up to the area and caught the tiny critter for us to observe. Even young, their mini tongue-less mouths full of ominous-looking teeth, I wanted my fingers nowhere near.

We also inner-tubed on the Amazon! The current swift, the rushing water bowled us under many times. I was lucky to escape with no scrapes, but a member of my party left with abrasions all along the left side of his body.

Packed days marked our time in this entire area. Some fished for one of the thirty-two species of ferocious piranha that inhabit the river. Others attended a concert at the improbable opera house of Manaus, built right in the middle of a jungle!

What a different experience to be up on deck for sunset and not hear the waves crashing into the sides of the ship! The water was too murky for sun to sparkle on it, but I would look out and see a lone man in his canoe. I wondered where he had just come from and what he was thinking as we glided by.

Chapter 42:

MOSCOW

I could not believe that I was finally seeing the Kremlin walls with my own two eyes, having grown up seeing them on the news everyday. "Reagan Meets Gorbachev Inside the Kremlin."

THE Kremlin, the ever-mysterious Kremlin…

Going to Moscow was another one of those unbelievable occasions where I was asked to help escort a sizable overland tour. Almost half of our cast was being replaced, though, and heavy rehearsals ate up our port time. I knew that the trip was an opportunity that I could not miss, so I pleaded for a day off from the woman brought onboard to run our arduous put-in rehearsals. Luckily, she recognized my opportunity and granted all of us veterans the day off in St. Petersburg while the newbies continued rehearsal.

Yay!

The tour lasted thirteen hours. Our passports readied, we formed a dutiful line, barging our way off the ship and through customs. We had priority that morning since our flight had to be caught.

In Moscow, we boarded our bus for the day and met our guide. I sat in the back with our St. Petersburg guide; she knew a lot about Moscow, too, so I basically ended up with my own private informant!

Moscow is incredibly clean, unlike St. Pete's. I was very surprised by this, but it is the capital city, after all. I had wrongly assumed that ALL of Russia was still adjusting to its new government. Also unlike St. Pete's, Moscow did not seem as easily walkable, but I was in a bus, without a map in front of me.

The Kremlin is a huge fortress. I had no idea. I thought the Kremlin was like the White House, something on a much smaller scale. Russia is apparently loaded with kremlins, the one in Moscow the best preserved.

Our guide (and the tour description) had warned us not to bring any large bags. They are strictly forbidden in the Kremlin. I pared down my necessary items for the next few hours and placed them into my camera case. Most of the passengers followed suit. However, one woman brought a collapsible cloth bag with her that the very serious guards would not allow her to bring in. There was nothing in it, and the woman looked about as innocent as anyone imaginable. The bag cleverly made its way to the back of the line where my guide rolled it up just to save time and trauma. One guard, though, highly astute, discovered this ploy (probably seeing it everyday), and would not budge on his decision to ban it. For some odd reason, this woman could not part with the stupid thing that she probably got for free by joining some nature magazine.

Becoming quite a nuisance, precious time ticked away. "My" guide tried to push her way past the hefty guard, but he just stuck out his chest and stepped right in her way! I could not believe the power struggle going on here over a couple square feet of canvas. Finally, she gave in and abandoned the ridiculous thing.

Seven wasted minutes...

What a treat to see the museum of the Armoury Chamber in the Kremlin! I viewed Peter the Great's enormous boots, Katherine the Great's wedding dress, Ivan the Terrible's throne and ermine-lined crown, and an elaborate tea set given to the tsars from Napoleon. Items on display glittered with emeralds. I had just learned that more of the Faberge eggs would be back in their homeland after being housed for so long in New York at the Forbes Galleries. To me, like the Elgin Marbles, it seems only right that certain pieces of cultural value should return to the country of their creation.

We stopped in the cathedral decorated with astonishing gold mosaics where all of the old tsars of Russia were crowned and later buried. The last tsar and his family, more recently recovered, rest in St. Petersburg.

We lunched directly off of Red Square. Of course the most delicious borscht ever was our appetizer, with beef Stroganoff our entrée. Everyone seemed quite happy with the meal and our whirlwind trip continued to Red Square itself and the fantastical St. Basil's Cathedral.

Extremely limited with time, I did not enter the cathedral, and unfortunately, Red Square was closed the day of our visit. I did not have to worry about whether or not I'd get in to view Mr. Lenin's tomb.

Another surreal experience was seeing this great space completely empty.

Loads of vendors stood by the cathedral selling postcards and I indulged, my first opportunity to stop and shop for a moment. Fuzz from the poplar trees blew everywhere that day, like snow, and my guide shared with me how her teenaged daughter was too young to remember the Communist days. She used to have to wait in long lines for bread. I was surprised to witness how busy and colorfully clothed everyone here was, a far cry from what I had grown up observing on television.

My group toured the cavernous underground system, too. The metro stations, surprisingly clean, lit up with exquisite chandeliers! We could smell chocolate being produced across the river as we waited to gather everyone back up. Unfortunately, a trip to the factory was not on our itinerary.

Admiring a colorful bed of red flowers at the side of the road, I spotted an ad for Cher's concert that night! A life-long fan, I had never seen her live. What irony that we'd be "together" in Moscow, Russia for a day, yet I unable to indulge.

We boarded our plane and returned safely to the ship, where a Russian cultural show was underway. The day was not quite over yet and my head was still spinning from all of the rich history packed into a few frenetic hours.

Chapter 43:

MOM!

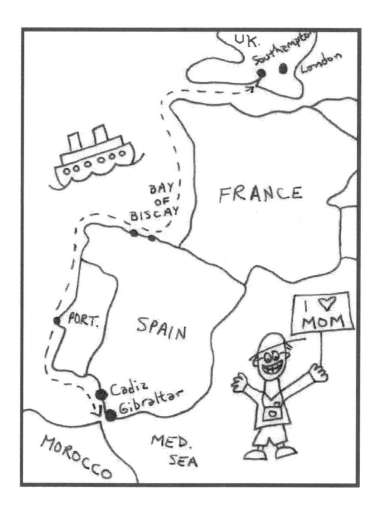

The monkey sat on my mother's head...

When I found out that I was going to be on the Cunard Caronia for one whole year, my Mom and her boyfriend Joe immediately booked a cruise so that we would see one another. However, I was a bit nervous about her fitting in with the generally older and British ship's passengers. How would they handle my younger, hip, American mama?

She fit in fine.

I did have to act as her interpreter at dinner when the neighboring Scot was just being friendly and asking how her "dee" went. My ear was pretty much attuned to the myriad accents onboard by then, but Mom lives in homogenized upstate New York. The most exotic patois there is the Canadian "eh".

Mom and Joe had a few days in London to get over their jetlag and enjoy the city. Then they rode the train to Southampton where I had to meet them. This was tricky. I only had a general time for when they'd be coming to the station. A few trains came and went. No Mom and Joe.

The suspense!

Had they gotten lost? Were they even in the country? I didn't know anything.

Another train pulled in. The doors opened and out popped my mother in her funky leather jacket. I was right there in front of her, but with my new haircut she didn't recognize me! Had it been that long?

After our joyous reunion, we had a delicious pub lunch and experienced the Queen's English together at Hog's Head. I had ordered a chicken wrap and soda. Our waiter asked, "Ice and a slice?" Confused, I repeated my request, thinking that he heard me order a slice of pizza! I'd been with Brits for a long time by this point, but never heard that "ice and a slice" meant a cold soda with a slice of lemon! I just assumed my drink would come with ice, but apparently, we Americans prefer it much more than those British blokes.

Mom got a kick out of seeing the phone in the welcome lounge that I called her from internationally. After their effortless check-in, I was instantly transformed into their personal cruise director. I knew the ship and its daily events better than my name and had been to most of the ports, too, so everything was planned stress-free for my two new favorite passengers.

Settled into their tiny cabin (with champagne from the Hotel Manager!), Mom booked her beauty treatments, presents from me. She had never had a manicure!

The next day at sea, Mom was getting her morning massage. We were in the Bay of Biscay, notoriously rocky during that time of year. Mom's masseuse was brand new not only to our ship, but ships in general. And terribly seasick. Mom was lying there on the little table, trying to relax on her first day of the cruise, and the poor masseuse was behind a very thin door losing everything from her Irish tummy.

Bless her heart.

Mom rescheduled. Thank goodness I had forced her and Joe to take their seasick pills. (I gave them crew pills. Hush, hush...the passenger ones make you D-R-O-W-S-Y...)

Mom is a big ham and it took no convincing to get her to participate in the fashion show a few days later. I was her partner. The beauty salon always gave the passengers in the show free hair styling and Mom called me and Joe when she was done with her appointment, excited as a little girl on Christmas morning: they had straightened her super-curly hair.

By now, everyone knew that my mother was onboard. At the opening night introductions, I told everyone to treat her like the queen that she is! And they did! Mom was a mini celebrity onboard and I know she loved every moment.

Before this time, all the performing that I'd done on ships had to be viewed by her at home on video. Now she finally watched live, arriving early to sit in the front row, and enduring all of our rehearsals, too. She and Joe became cast groupies for ten days!

I think our most memorable side trip together was in Gibraltar. We hired a local guy to take us up the Rock to visit the caves, fortresses, and of course, the famous Barbary apes. I had seen them many times, but always enjoyed returning for more. Mom was admiring one of their tiny dark hands and perfect little fingernails when suddenly, looking over at other tourists, she said, " I want one of them on my head".

I almost fell over.

This was from a woman who would run over to the next county if a little dog jumped up on her to lick her face in eager greeting. This was from a woman deathly afraid of mice.

I was standing there thinking about all of the heads this ape had been on, the ticks infesting its fur and I was frozen, just agape that my mother so casually wanted to become intimate with this feral beast. But she stressed, "How many times am I going to be in Gibraltar with my son? Put it on my head." Our driver quickly obeyed. Mom was so into it, she had TAKEN OFF HER EARRINGS! Soon, Joe had a furry friend on his head, too.

Dammit, I was still thinking of the skin disease that I would catch from these things, fun enough to watch, but I couldn't be a big wuss if Joe and Mom had become so bold.

So, in the end, yes, the indifferent ape conquered my head, too.

From Cadiz, Spain, we took the tour to Jerez, the land of Tio Pepe sherry. Our guide was named Carmen. I had escorted this very same tour four years prior and Carmen happened to be my guide back then! I noticed that she seemed to be sadder than I had remembered. And I honestly did remember her because there was a silly photo of us taken with the sombrero-ed Tio Pepe girl that I got to keep for my scrapbook.

A gorgeous ride through the beautiful countryside to Jerez, the tourist-friendly facilities at the bodega allowed us to sample five kinds of sherry. We also observed the alcoholic mice living in the storage area full of huge raisin-smelling barrels.

A glass of sherry placed out for the mice, there is a little ladder that they climb (no lie!) to sip the good stuff! Does PETA España know about this? Nonetheless an entertaining sight, we kept Mom at a safe distance.

As we climbed back onto the bus, I introduced Carmen to my Mom. The two said their hellos and as I did my last check outside to make sure that nobody from my bus was lingering, Carmen leaned over to me and said, "Enjoy your mother while she's here. I just lost mine this winter."

Thank you, Carmen. I will.

Chapter 44:

SURPRISE!

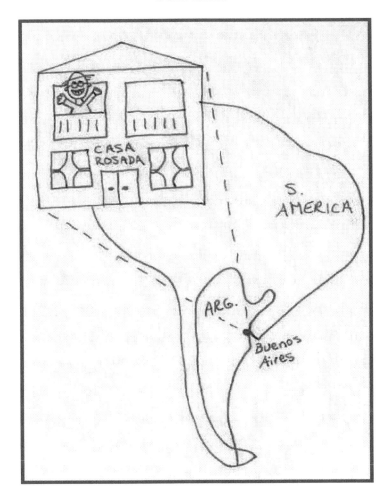

The best thing about travel is its potential for surprise. One tour that I escorted in particular was loaded with a non-stop amount of it—The Argentine Fiesta Gaucha. Our hosts of Estancia La Fortuna went all out for us on this day, perpetuating this popular tour's reputation. Three of us from the production cast made the trek out onto the pampas and became royalty along with our passengers.

Our buses pulling into the ranch, horsemen dressed in full martial gear atop their well-groomed pintos accompanied us in. Hundreds of pounds of steak, chicken, and ribs sizzled from within an open barbeque pit, stacked on an enormous grill or inside little metallic cages placed right near the embers. Visiting the area later to take photos, the two gentlemen in charge of the meat allowed us to "tend" the ashes with their long hoes, a very important job!

Refreshed with drinks and empanadas, mini bites of beef or chicken baked in dough, we next took a short carriage ride around the beautiful grounds of the ranch. Stately trees grew in an expansive grassy area, providing welcome amounts of shade. I saw myself coming back for an extended stay, living in one of the many outbuildings tucked away in its own private copse.

We got to horseback ride, too. Stunning and regal, the horses' coats shone brilliantly in the powerful sun. I could just tell that my steed knew I had no clue how to handle it.

At mealtime, course after course was piled upon our table. We thought we would explode, sampling all of the meat offered, cooked to juicy perfection, and enjoying vibrant salads, too. Bolo dancers entertained us with their dizzying speed, deftly dodging their pieces of leather with heavy wooden beads attached at the end. The dancers swung the bolos around dangerously and hit the floor rhythmically while pounding their heeled boots. I imagined myself attempting this, picturing two black eyes and some horrifying form of self-strangulation.

Many birds sang throughout the gorgeous day, and I snuck from the group to discover five new species for my world list! Armed with a guidebook, I was a kid in a candy store, finding and identifying my little, colorful treasures.

The horses then raced, kicking up dirt and relentlessly pounding the earth. A couple brave souls sat Indian-style on a cowhide "sled" attached to one of the horses and got pulled for a dusty distance behind! That looked like a lot of fun, but I was too busy identifying a rufous hornero and saffron finch!

This day was a far cry from the previous one I'd spent in Buenos Aires. I ran myself ragged, visiting each neighborhood and taking in all of the sights, especially interested in those having to do with Eva Peron. Several decades later, the utterance of her name produces heated opinions and controversy. Our day in the country provided no asphalt or tension.

Finally, our visit wrapped up. Two hours and fifteen minutes stretched out ahead of us on the road back to the ship. The ranch gave polo shirts to us escorts (another perk!) as if the day had not been memorable enough. Many unexpected pleasures filled this tour, making for several happy thoughts as we traveled back into the bustling city.

Chapter 45:

FREE AS THE BREEZE

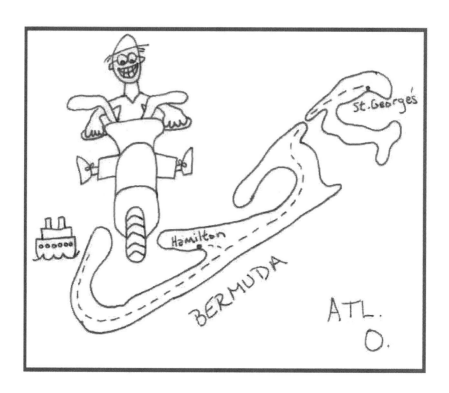

Scooters!

Our last time in Bermuda, three cast members and I found out that within the naval yard where we tied up, scooters were available for rent. My driving skills are quite unpolished, at best, but my partner couldn't drive at all, so I acquired full command. The other driver and I donned our helmets, had quick lessons (which we passed!), and zoomed off for our day on the road.

My partner and I had quite a time coordinating our take-off. At first, we thought that we needed to push off together and then put up our feet to safety, but inevitably, our timing was off and her foot ended up dragging. Then we figured that she needed to settle first (tricky for me balance-wise), before I steered out onto the barren road, always waiting for no oncoming traffic due to my still-questionable ability. The handlebars held the controls for the brakes and gas, so I had to adjust to my feet doing nothing except pushing off.

Now I understand why some folks love their motorcycles so much. These little things did not go as fast, but the wind on my face and the open road in front of us sold me anyway. Bermuda is a pastel-colored and palm tree-laden isle; the full day was ours to enjoy its sights. The rental price reasonable, gasoline going a long way, and with two people splitting costs, we ended up with an efficient and fun activity to pass the day with. Ours was a groundbreaking choice. We zipped by all of the crew, they saw how much fun we were having, and by the end of the day, many more had rented these handy things.

Hardly alone amongst the locals, we struggled to find spaces in the "scooter parking lot" when we broke for lunch in Hamilton. Cars tolerated us. We just pulled over a lot to allow the patient autos clearance.

I happened to be the only American amongst my group of three Brits, so my "game" was to speak with their accent all day. How did I do? Would 'Enry 'Iggins 'ave been proud or were my mates just indulging a silly American boy and rolling their six eyes behind my enthusiastic back?

The jury is still out on that one.

Our goal for the day was to tootle over to St. George's, all the way across the island. We did that with no problems, but it took a great while. I had a bit of a scrape turning the moped around quickly. I couldn't do an easy three-point turn somehow and had to humbly ask my girl (AKA "Biker Chick") to climb off for a moment.

That was so uncool.

The nicest thing about arriving in town finally was parking the scooter and having to remember where it was. Such responsibility! Lunching in Hamilton, we overlooked our scooters, assuring that they were OK. After posing for pictures in St. George's stockyard, we had a bit of a snack: strawberry cheesecake and a nice spot of tea (I was fitting in "brilliantly" with my Brits).

While leaving St. George's, I suffered another blow to my easy riding ego. I took my scooter off of its kickstand before getting the balance right. It toppled right over with me, a flummoxed helmeted heap on top. Quickly looking about to see if I had been spied, alas, I had been! But the situation was far worse than having just been merely observed. A friend was right there with her camera, as though this whole scene had been planned, my ineptitude preserved forever on film.

Does Bermuda advertise pink sands? As the sun set, we paid a quick visit to Elbow Beach. Now call it too much air, or the angle of the sun, but the sand was not pink. Has it faded over the years? If not, we were at the wrong beach and/or the latest victims of false advertising. Nonetheless, the sun was lowering, the air suddenly chilling us.

Strangely, stupidly, most of us only wore shorts this whole day. We did not even consider the danger of being out on the road without any leg protection. This is not recommended. Luckily nothing happened to any of us, but what a serious oversight! Practically shaking with cold by the time we returned to our port in the dark (also not recommended), again, pants would've been nice.

That was not the end of scooter time for me. I had not had nearly enough. I ate my dinner and climbed back onto my new toy, still half full of petrol! We didn't have to replenish the tank before returning it, either. I felt even freer riding around alone, once I found my new balance, but also somewhat lonely. I ended up chauffeuring different members of the crew as they came off of the ship and made their way to a nearby bar that had stayed open for us on our overnight stay.

Why did I love this day so much? What was it about the scooter that set me soaring? Perhaps it reminded me of the excitement that I felt as a kid when I was on a bicycle and in control of myself, rather than dependant on Mom and Dad. Perhaps I was simply delirious with joy to be off of the ship after two or three days at sea in a confined space. My company that day was excellent, all of us silly and carefree. I don't think we talked shop for one minute. Mostly, I believe it was the potential of the open road. Bermuda is a small island, yes, but we had no idea where we were going. It was a "follow-the-signs" kind of day, where we had no time constraints, and no expectations.

Chapter 46:

DELIRIOUS FROM THE HEAT

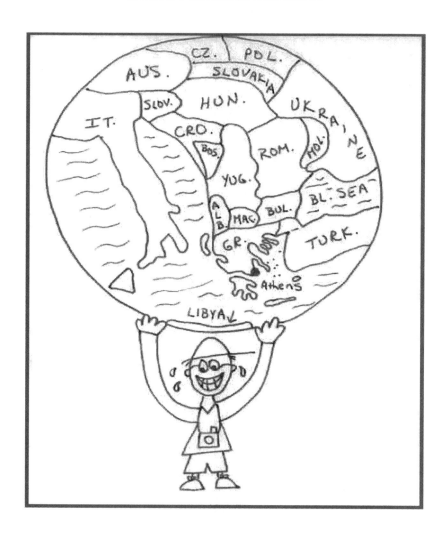

Greece!

Besides Egypt, this country was the destination that I longed to visit most as a kid. The mythological histories of both countries had me under their spell and I devoured every book possible to learn more about their gods and goddesses.

In Piraeus, Greece, four busloads of passengers took the tour to the Parthenon. An enormous ship next to us had about twenty-five buses doing the same thing while other ships docked near us, too. It was going to be crowded.

And hot.

So hot.

My-sneakers-are-melting hot.

Even in the early morning hours, the heat and humidity enveloped the hundreds of us at the "new" amphitheater, built in 1896, capable of holding 70,000 spectators for the first modern Olympics.

Several on my tour had already opted to stay onboard for this destination. We next arrived at stop number two. The ascent up to the Acropolis began and one by one, due to the heat and physical challenges involved, more members of my group informed me that they'd meet us back at the bus. Those remaining climbed the narrow steps up to the magnificent plateau of Athens' most famous site. No order existed within any group, tangled in with the next, the guides giving commentary to a bunch of random tourists. This was an escort's nightmare.

And did I mention the heat?

My dwindling party snaked its way to the top of the Acropolis. I was completely preoccupied by avoiding stepping on any one of the many pastel-clad visitors sitting around ON THE STEPS hording the scant bit of shade. All of my video footage contained tourists. I was here to see the Parthenon, of course, but this was a far from ideal situation, even with the perk of not having to pay for the trip. The whole experience was becoming a bit of a let down, but I took in all of the information possible and just figured that someday, I'd have to come back.

After the tour, at lunch back on the ship, I realized that I could just go back that day! Ever the opportunist, my ticket was still valid and I had ample time in the afternoon!

The train station sat a thirty-minute walk away from the ship. The congested harbor of Piraeus contained the countless ferries dispatching their passengers to the three hundred inhabited Greek island gems. The train was easy to figure out, even with Greek signage, and ran frequently. I was spewed out into Athens once again, but this time on my own.

By now the temperature was at its peak, the heavy air of an overheated oven. At 40° C (104° F), sweat poured out of my head, soaking my cap with even the slightest exertion. Thank goodness for my water bottle.

Weaving my lethargic way through the dense Plaka district full of markets and weary vendors, I somehow found my way back to the Acropolis.

It was empty!

Though insane to be there at that oppressive time in the afternoon, this was the Acropolis I had imagined: isolated, quiet, and powerful. Looking up at the Parthenon and seeing it stand alone in its grandeur made my trip back there immediately worthwhile. I noticed different colors of marble, signifying where repairs had been made over the millennia. The path actually spread before me as I approached again, unburdened from my escort duties.

My imagination ran on overdrive in this ruined place. So much time had passed with the marble enduring so much change and looking as if leprosy had set in, eroding all edges. If those corroded and chipped columns could talk! What was the air like when the Parthenon was brand new? Certainly cleaner. What did those ancient people wear and eat? What scents wafted in the air? Was the ground smoother?

I indulged in the vistas from the Acropolis. Modern Athens invades the fading ruins. A car parked right by a fallen column, its pieces a used run of dominoes, didn't make sense. Other columns rose up incompletely, their capitals having long ago disintegrated. Many temples and scraps of rotting marble littered the grounds amidst modern day structures that suffocated antiquity like an unrelenting lava flow. At the theater of Dionysus, the upper seating level was returning back to Mother Earth right before my eyes, ancient names carved into the marble seats barely legible.

The museum up near the Parthenon, air-conditioned and included in the price of admission, preserved the actual statuary left on the Acropolis from acid rain. Priceless pieces of friezes sat out on display, their missing parts painted onto the wall, completing the puzzle. Some remnants still contained tinges of original color, reminding me that the Parthenon was not always a bleached skeleton of rock. Around a corner laid a torso, then a hand, dismembered cruelly from its god-like body.

My experience of the Acropolis had completely changed. I bought my requisite souvenir booklet after browsing the exhibits and knew that soon it was time to be brave and return to the oven, the stifling land once ruled by gods.

Chapter 47:

FALLING IN LOVE...MUTUALLY... WITH SOMEBODY WHILE AT SEA

Chapter 48:

PASSENGERS

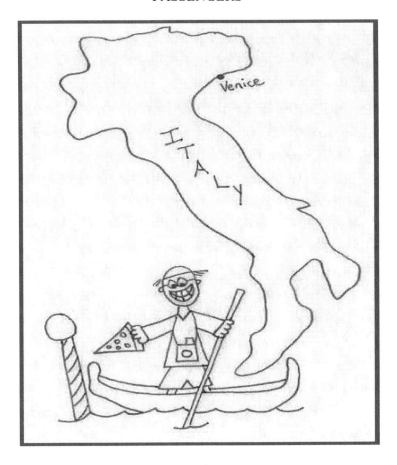

I approach a single woman at the Captain's Cocktail Party. She looks lonely. I'll chat with her.

She looks me up. She looks me down.

"I do NOT want to talk to you."

Next…

Part of my job was to meet as many passengers as possible and help make their cruise a pleasant experience. Doesn't sound like too bad a job, right? Reread the above. It really happened to me.

On the other hand, once I was making my way to the ballroom on the Rotterdam and I passed two elderly women who had clearly been drinking. They had looked me over and made some kind of comment to me and for some reason I had to return and pass them again. As I approached, one fully said out loud to the other, "Mm, well isn't HE cute!" This was not a grandmotherly affection. It sounded quite salacious, something one would hear in "Cocoon".

One lady walked everywhere on the Caronia rolling a day bag with her, as if a stewardess onto her next flight. Everybody, crew and passengers alike, wondered what she kept in the thing, but nobody to my knowledge, ever found out.

My last time in Venice, a friend and I had the privilege of being escorted around by two Norwegians who knew the intricate city quite impressively. They maneuvered their way around and amazed us with their knowledge of the best non-touristy places to eat and have a cappuccino. Our lunch stop had such great business from us that its proprietors let us sample four varieties of their homemade liqueur!

Pulling into port late one morning, I was on the gangway waiting to greet everyone as they disembarked for the day. This frazzled woman burst into the area speaking very loudly. She had obviously just woken up. Her hair was tussled, her shorts on crooked, and she was afraid of missing her tour. I assured her that nobody had debarked yet, but she was adamant that I was lying to her and insisted I let her off! Suddenly, as if reality had hit her dead in the face, she looked down at herself perplexedly and asked, "Well, am I dressed?" I had to leave the area, I was laughing so hard, as were several other fully cognizant passengers.

A generous couple wanted to TIP us for our performance. That was a nice surprise.

On the Sun, we had a couple that would throw huge parties for the crew and give everybody tee shirts. They would invite us up to their penthouse for dinner parties, too. Another man donated money to the crew welfare that was used to throw a huge cross-dressing theme party for us. (By the way, some guys just don't look pretty in a dress, especially when trying on heels for the first time on a moving ship!) This same man gave the cast so much champagne after our shows that the supply lasted for months after he had gone.

At the end of the South America cruise, a couple gave me two engraved wine glasses that they didn't have room for in their suitcases. Perfect timing! It happened to be my birthday that night. Being America-bound, they kindly mailed some postcards for me.

One evening, I had been speaking with a doctor and his wife and we realized that not only was he from my hometown, but he also worked at the same hospital as my mother! Imagine her surprise upon arriving to her office that next Monday and finding a note from me on her desk hand-delivered by this kind man! Coincidentally, a year or so later, we cruised and conspired again together, much to Mom's delight.

I enjoyed seeing our repeat cruisers on the Caronia. After a whole year onboard, I got to know many of them. It was always a pleasure to recognize the familiar face of somebody who was happy to see that I was there, too.

Chapter 49:

BEHEMOTH AT SEA

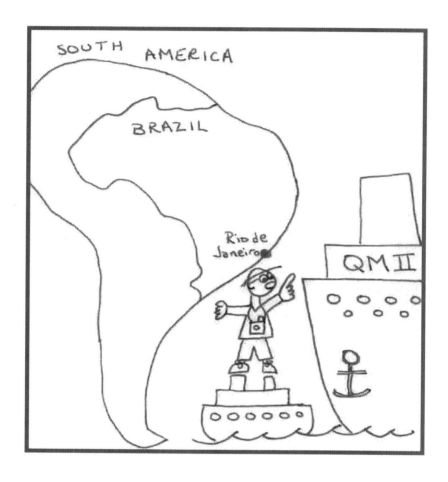

Queen Mary II hoopla has set in. One of our highest-ranking officers
has become land-based in order to oversee the construction of Cunard's
newest project. More and more bulletins are posted in the office about
the keel being laid or the bridge being assembled, and lecturers are
onboard to glorify its specs--too wide to traverse the Panama Canal!
The crew is briefed on what life will be like on the QMII...

Slowly losing crew, transferred over to the bigger ship, the day came for its christening. I first saw the Queen Mary II at the QEII terminal in Southampton and, boy, was she big! The top of our ship lined up with the roof of the terminal; the QMII's hull alone came up to the same place! Our ship looked as if it were sinking next the massive structure.

I still can't get over, for as long as I have sailed, that somebody can construct and assemble tons of heavy STEEL, enabling it to float. That being said, this ship was twice the size of the Queen Elizabeth II and six times the size of the Caronia, making it truly the tallest, widest, heaviest, yet fastest ship afloat.

I was not able to board the behemoth until we shared the dock in Rio de Janeiro, Brazil. Allowed access as fellow Cunarders, it was a great privilege to see this vessel while still fresh and crisp. The library alone blew me away with its row upon row of shelving and diverse selection, including an impressive array of birding books! The attendant there informed us that it took a half hour just to unlock all of the cabinets! We also learned that the crew could call home from their cabins, a BIG deal for ship life, eliminating the need for the next port and inevitable long lines at payphones.

An endless amount of lounges were available (a champagne lounge, a cigar lounge), and several hard-to-find places to lose yourself, kind of like how I felt on the old Rotterdam. The stage impressed us with its state-of-the-art sound system and multiple moving platforms, as did the planetarium. Imagine! A planetarium at sea! There was a British pub to stop into for a pint and a two-story disco that never had to double as another space during the day.

Enjoying the extensive artwork and reading the historical Cunard facts with accompanying photos could have occupied my whole day—a museum at sea. The ship's design included tender lounges in order to accommodate the passengers who waited to board them. We joked that the Caronia was one of the QMII's tenders.

The beauty salon was airy and bright and like the disco, two stories tall, as was the main dining room, a stunning array of balconies and spiraling staircases. The shops took over a whole deck, instead of two tiny rooms, and the pool area, to die for with whirlpools everywhere, included a full lunch grill with a retractable sunroof. Oh, and don't forget the helipad, truly making this ship a floating city.

I appreciated seeing the Queen Mary II, I really did. I enjoyed its inner décor and beautiful layout, but to me, bigger is not always better. I was very content to return to my cozy Caronia, sailing on to the next port of call that beckoned.

Chapter 50:

VIDEOTAPING

As we toured Australia and Asia together, my friend Brent recorded
priceless footage on his video camera. I realized then the value of his
product, while I was limited to still photography. On an African safari
later, I bought his same exact camera and videoed just about every
moment of that trip. The camera proved to be very durable, functioning

fine after being dropped a few times and surviving a car accident unscathed.

It came with me on the Caronia during my first six months there, so by the end of that year, I had used my video camera almost everyday for seven months! And it held up beautifully, highlighted with scratches, dents, and other field wounds.

My technique, however, needed work. Every time I zoomed in on a subject, I'd make an annoying noise as if racing at the Indianapolis 500. That got old once I started reviewing my footage. I'd also get confused and tape when I meant to be resting the machine. Too much footage shows the sideways view of where I was walking to next.

My friend Suzannah was putting together a highlights tape of our European adventures to show her family and brought my favorite subjects to attention: cute kids, animals, and flowers. My camera allowed me to film people without their knowing, sneaking footage of striking clothes that Africans wore in the airport, for instance.

The camera got me into trouble, too. Filming a walking tour of my ship to show friends and family, I came up to the glass doors of our little casino. The manager stormed over to me throwing a fit, which ended up being the best part of my tape! Who knew that a ship's casino would be off-limits, yet I could get away with filming inside the Sistine Chapel? Photos and videos are strictly prohibited there, but I managed to capture quite a bit of footage with my subversive machine. Its design enabled the image to be seen on a screen, rather than through a telltale viewfinder.

In order for our dance captain to give us dance notes, we had to tape all of our rehearsals. I started compiling our funny mistakes onto a blooper reel, cause for the cast to get together and roar at the latest additions to our ever-growing compilation.

My camera bag became my "purse", holding my money, sunscreen, and phone cards. Going everywhere that I did, it was almost stolen from me in Malaga, Spain. Some men came up to me and asked where the ocean was! I fell for their distracting ploy, naively trying to help them. Luckily, a pickpocket expert had just been onboard. Sure enough, I turned back around and saw their buddy walking away with my camera bag, filing through it and looking for money. Uncharacteristically bold, I walked right over to him, grabbed my bag back, and said, "Nice try". Of course, there was not a police officer in sight.

I grew quite attached to my video camera. But by year number two and a half, the poor thing would only work after literally giving it a rigorous shake, to the bemusement of my peers. Tiny loose parts could be heard jangling around inside the silver shell, but my irreverent technique granted the camera a few more months of life.

Finally, three and a half years after its purchase, my beloved camera completely expired. I couldn't even play my tapes anymore. Traveling all over the world with me, that camera captured some of my best memories.

Chapter 51:

KAYAKING

Why do I find lighthouses so alluring? Perhaps it's their power to shine through the strongest fog, or their ability to withstand the fiercest of elements. They sprout from craggy rocks, beautiful reminders of pre-radar life at sea.

From Sitka, Alaska, three cast members and I rented two kayaks and paddled all over the area where the ships anchored. Sitka is a port within the southeastern arm of the big state and when we anchored off the coast of the actual town, the density of the surrounding pine-covered islands gave the feeling that the ship had been magically transported onto a large northern lake. Eagles perched everywhere in Sitka, as numerous as gulls on a beach. Two juveniles flew right over my head one day in the forest. I could feel the displaced air of their silent, yet eerie wing beats on my head.

Our kayaking instructor briefed us on safety and proper paddling before we enthusiastically kicked away from the dock. Despite the chilly, overcast day, oaring quickly warmed up our muscles.

Soon, the lofty goal of kayaking to our ship, the ss Rotterdam, was abandoned as we realized that it was anchored too far away. Instead, we glided our way over to the picturesque red and white lighthouse that guarded the area's waters. Like hiking, we worked for a tangible goal.

Closer and closer to our little beacon we saw a couple lounging around at its base. We gave them a friendly wave and before we knew it, were invited not only to stop for a much-needed rest, but also take a peek inside!

Our hosts welcomed us to climb up through the small trapdoor in the tower to see the rustic sleeping accommodations. The romantic lighthouse was cottage-like, built of wood slat walls and containing beds with warm, wooly blankets. All of the appropriate Alaskan décor completed its look. My friends and I enjoyed the delightful space, but out of earshot, past the ominous trap, we joked about this being the perfect set up for our grisly murders. Very vulnerable, nobody from the ship knew our whereabouts, and we had never seen people here before (or after, either). Luckily, our active imaginations were all that plotted dastardly deeds that day.

Soon after, we glided off again, "arm ache" officially setting in as the rain started down. The occupants of the other kayak had had enough for the day, but happily for me, my oaring partner was willing to continue our mini tour. The Sagafjord was sharing the harbor with us and we paddled around it. Strangely enough, this vessel was the sister ship of the Vistafjord that I later sailed on for two years as the Cunard Caronia.

Exhausted and drenched, we pulled ourselves back to the dock, thoroughly exercised. I looked over to the lighthouse, fading into the mist.

Chapter 52:

RENEGADES PART III: PARIS

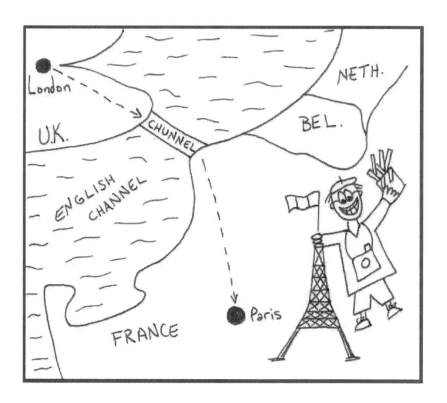

The plan was perfect!

Cunard allowed its employees to extend their time in Europe for a vacation before flying home. I took advantage of this by revisiting two of my favorite cities.

I lived in London for a semester. Returning after many years, plenty of new sites awaited: the Eye, the wonderful new Globe Theatre, the Millennium Bridge, and sadly, the Princess Diana Memorial Walk in Kensington Park. The Chunnel had been under construction during my months there, so this time, I indulged in the convenient ride to Paris, saving hours of travel and cutting transfer hassles exponentially.

My ship pal, Brent, met me there. He was working as a dancer at the famed Lido. His goofy sense of humor matches mine and we both delve right into foreign destinations to acquaint ourselves as best we can. We harassed one another over who was geekier: me for carrying around a dictionary or him for meticulously journaling everything?

Europe was in the middle of the worst heat wave it had ever experienced. Sultry New York City summers well under my belt, I didn't feel much difference, but Parisians were grossly unprepared. An electric fan for sale could not be found and those without air conditioning suffered.

Brent and I decided one afternoon to tour the Paris Opera House. A fan of The Phantom of the Opera (book and musical!), I enjoyed the legends surrounding its haunted past. We joked about finding the underground lake and getting a personal tour from Mr. Phantom himself.

We were not so far off…

The site was a popular destination that day, the semi-cool building a refreshing and stunning respite. The lobby alone was spectacular enough, but we purchased a full tour, including access to the actual theater, where I pictured the great chandelier crashing down and doing its damage.

Wandering about and being our silly selves, we came upon an unassuming door that we thought we'd try. It was open and nobody stopped us. Ordinarily, the stuffiness of a non-cooled area would indicate its not being part of the tour. Did this make us pause?

No.

We entered a wide labyrinth, halls twisting and turning every few steps.

We scaled stairwells thick with stale air and peeked everywhere that we could. Through dingy round windows, the rest of Paris steamed beyond the bronze roofing that highlighted this ornate building.

Before we knew it, we appeared in the catwalks OVER the stage! How did we do that? By trespassing, yes, but this opportunity was too rich to be paranoid about. If caught, we could either play "dumb tourists" (see RENEGADES PART II: HONOLULU) or, with his so-so French, mon ami could talk us out of a dreaded night in the modern day equivalent of the Bastille.

Even we drew the line at walking out onto the catwalks. Their incredible height was beyond dizzying. A few pieces of scenery lay around, but my goal was to find the costume shop.

By now, "down" was our only option. Why not try to discover the underground? Along the way, we found a whole floor of rehearsal spaces. What fun to imagine all of the dancers and singers through time perfecting their moments onstage. We saw the rooms built with raked floors so that the performers could adjust to the odd sensation before working on the actual stage boards. I could almost still smell sweat in the heavy air.

By this point, Brent and I actually became smug for having seen so much and not gotten caught. But suddenly, voices and distant footsteps approached. Our hearts raced and we debated over whether to run or just face our grim fates. We banked on our innocence and just pressed on. Advancing towards the still-unseen figures, up some odd staircase in the middle of a floor, we met two men who looked like maintenance workers. They gave us a quick look, Brent nodded his head and they walked right by. They didn't even care!

If we had been smug BEFORE...

They probably just thought of us as new members of the corps de ballet checking the place out. Brent actually had his dance bag with him, so we didn't look that out-of-place.

Strangely, once "caught", our steam fizzled. We didn't find any costumes, but ended up in the administrative part of the building just as we began wondering how to get out of the place. The time had come to submit ourselves not only back into the heat, but also fresher air. Would the ladies in these offices prove our worst obstacle, questioning us mercilessly before we could pass?

Nah.

They didn't care about us, either.

We remained calm until turning the next corner along the cobbled streets, gloating geeks who had REALLY gotten their money's worth.

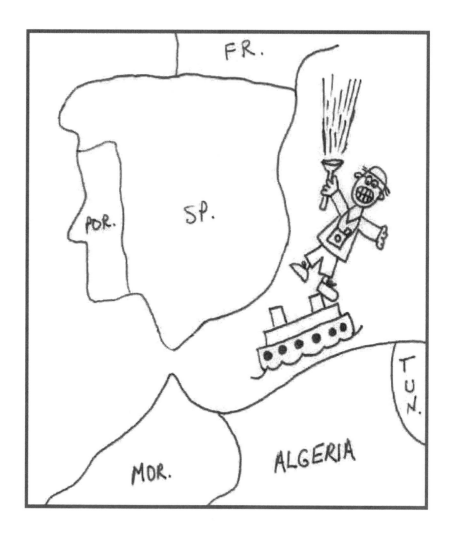

Our lead male vocalist was opening the show for somebody that night.

A very talented singer and entertainer, he had just sung a few of his hits and was starting another. Suddenly, his microphone died and the spotlight went out. His unamplified voice boomed out with, "Hey, I wasn't THAT bad, was I?" The audience chuckled at his improv as wonderment started to set in. What was going on? The ballroom was full of six hundred people in the dark, both physically and mentally.

Our cruise director's job became very interesting at this point. Between calling up to the bridge to inform the captain of the major power outage underway, he also had to keep an anxious crowd happy. Our brilliant vocalist put to use his ad-libbing skills and lead a well-received sing along! Meanwhile, with no air conditioning, the ballroom gradually heated up and passengers began to get antsy and leave.

Thank goodness for a nice clear night outside with a calm sea and nearly full moon. Off the coast of Algeria, my mind took comfort in seeing the lights of the land just in case this turned out to be a disaster of some sort. Although, what could I have done, jumped overboard and attempted to swim? How many miles from land did we bob around, really, those lights in the distance just a misleading tease?

By now, all of the other guest entertainers onboard (such good sports!) did their part to keep the crowd entertained. I was outside with the rest of the cast and most of the crew mingled on the deck right beneath us, just for some fresh air. Claustrophobia had reared its ugly head inside for us, but the ballroom buzzed with impromptu a cappela music and off-the-cuff entertainment. The emergency lights kicked on and we saw a man who had gone back to his room for his lifejacket! I suppose he could've been the one having the last laugh, but how odd is it to see a man in a tux wearing a hideous neon orange life jacket?

The Caronia started seriously listing to port, the most remarkable part of the night. At this point the captain finally came over the loudspeaker and told us what had happened.

The swimming pool in the gym had sprung a leak onto the ship's electric board and that excess water was throwing off the ballast, the balance of the ship! Dead on the water, a strange and RARE experience in the middle of the ocean, we went nowhere, heard and felt nothing. The enormous engines rumbled ever-present on that ship and to not feel or hear them was indeed unique. Assured that no other ships coursed around us at the time, a collision was not possible.

After about ninety minutes, the lights sprung back on and everybody outside gave a whooping cheer! Amazingly, the show that had been thrown into the dark went on as scheduled, even if one and a half hours late. Most of the audience had stuck the power failure out and finally retired at a very late (for them!) midnight.

Our itinerary had to be adjusted due to the lost time. Even after our power returned, we floated for quite a few hours. Our one stop in Corfu, Greece, was nixed but two days in Malta made up for it. Overnights always welcome, this was good news for the crew. Thankfully, the blackout ended up being just a minor little situation, but making for a memorable voyage. A cruise can be full of wonderful opportunities to discover new cultures and foods, but something like a blackout becomes the true highlight.

Some crewmembers had been caught in the shower when the lights went out. Our female singer was in the middle of dying her hair! These things are just bound to happen sometimes with self-contained living at sea.

Chapter 54:

IGNORANCE BE GONE!

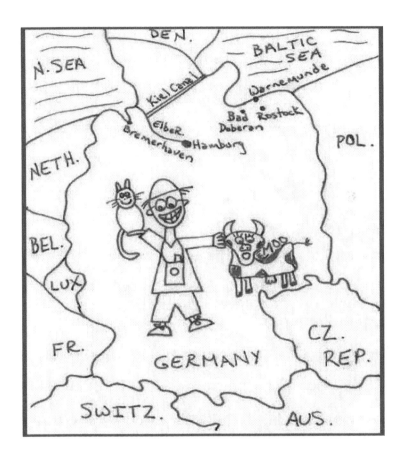

Stereotypes and fears are conquered by knowledge. That is the most valuable lesson I have learned from traveling.

I grew up fearing both Russia (as a child of the nuclear age) and Germany (ignorantly believing that little Hitlers still occupy the land!) Thankfully, because of my travels, I have grown to love both countries, especially Germany.

My first visit occurred during the dry dock experience in Bremerhaven described already. Despite our initial rough start, my Germanophilia had already begun to blossom.

The trolley tracks imbedded in the streets of Bremerhaven took me back to a more romantic time. A fruit and flower market was in full swing and our Hotel Haverkamp quaint and cozy, including a luxurious breakfast in the morning. It is silly, but I had never thought of Germany as "cozy" before this day. Sunlight streamed into my window as I woke up (the last time I would experience that for six months) and rich cathedral bells had chimed me into consciousness. A mellifluous bird sang loudly. We chose an American 50's style diner for our dinner that night (I must not have had a vote—why bother?) Rap songs in English, loaded with filthy words, blared from the jukebox! Nobody could have known the meanings of these words, becoming, ironically, the redeeming value of this eatery. We also noticed a lot of dubbed American TV. How strange that the American culture is so prevalent in Europe, when we are so Victorian in comparison.

Our German was extremely limited, yet friendly locals offered us a shortcut back to our hotel! We struggled the next morning to leave our last steady sleeping quarters for the next half-year.

The charming Kiel Canal brought us into Hamburg. The doors of its locks slid closed, not swung, like big brother's in Panama. Our day on the canal featured a "Count the Cows" contest for the passengers. Families on their bikes enjoyed rural recreation and waved to our Big Mama as she sailed by. A chorus of indigenous birds in the background hid within the brilliant greenery before us.

And hundreds of cows were counted.

A friend of mine worked in Hamburg and became my private guide. We met at the impressive Rathuis (an unfortunate name, yes, but literally "town hall"), and explored some nearby cathedral ruins leftover from World War II. She told me that with its numerous canals, Hamburg contains more water than Venice! We strolled to the theater where she was appearing in "Cats" and I was regaled with the German version of "Memory". My friend impressed me at dinner with her basic, but ample, German and then introduced me to the seedy Reeperbahn, a street definitely not for the prudish.

Having gone to Berlin during my first visit to Rostock, my only other experience there was in pouring rain during a "Great Internet Hunt" (very important on a ship). Our goal proved to be a challenging one to fulfill but, somehow, with international charades, we learned that a CLOTHING STORE held the nearest public computers.

OK.

A new brick-covered market area led us to our store and we bubbled up to find the coin-operated computers, like slot machines! Normally a set price is paid for a finite amount of e-mail time.

Not here.

"Plunk, plunk", went our euros...

Warnemunde ended up being my biggest surprise in Germany, clinching my love for all things Deutsch. Beginning with the Steam Nostalgia tour, we made a stop at a monastery in Bad Doberan, constructed of brick. An appealing mix of white plaster and red bricks decorated the interior while the grounds featured a separate tower of black brick highlights against terra cotta set in precise geometric patterns.

From there we boarded the "Molli" train, tiny and touristy, pulled by a steam locomotive through bucolic countryside. The short ride ended in a village called Heiligendamm and through some more charming roads, we rolled into the beach resort town of Kuehlungsborn. The Kaiser himself and the Russian tsars used to bathe there! After some refreshing apple cake, I had a little time to walk the beach.

Once back to the ship, I was thrilled to learn that the center of Warnemunde was within walking distance. I'd have time to check it out and go to the beach again! The boardwalk there sizzled, crammed with shoppers and seafarers enjoying summertime. The sight of German families conjured up my wonderful childhood memories of when we'd pack it up and travel somewhere for a fun getaway. The universal joy of this privilege surrounded me. I realized again that my previous ideas about Germany were all wrong. People have fun here!

I passed a few crewmembers sitting out and enjoying a nice lunch ashore, fantasized about owning a yacht, and somehow avoided the temptation to buy any number of sweets and carnival confections available. After all, I had had my apple cake.

Easily accessible, I was at the beach within minutes, realizing that nobody here cared about wearing clothes. My kind of beach! Young, old, single, or with families, nudity was not an issue here.

Our perfect weather had everybody in high spirits. Sailaway proved to be a very special one. German music played on shore as many, many people waved us farewell, quite a touching sight. Then I heard somebody calling my name! Who in the world knew me here?

My friend, who used to cut my hair in the ship's salon, had come to say "hello" and was amongst the crowd wishing us well through a sea of white hankies. Even though she was physically far away, it was sweet to remember the fun times that we shared on the ship together. I saw her wipe a tear from her eye.

That was my last visit to Germany, leaving an excellent impression full of joy and love. I am sad that I grew up thinking Germany was still full of concentration camps and anti-American sentiments. It was unfortunate thinking and fills me with shame, but luckily, it's in my past. Maybe someday I will visit Iraq or Afghanistan and grow unafraid of those countries as well. This is why travel is vital to all of mankind.

Chapter 55:

THE BEST SAIL-IN

Sailing into port can be an exciting occasion. The anticipation of what lies ahead is at its peak. Early birds caught the sail-ins and though I was usually not one of them, sometimes I just had to rouse myself because that caliber of scenery did not present itself everyday.

What was my best sail-in?

Could it have been San Francisco? The morning was a pretty bittersweet one. Excited to view the Golden Gate Bridge in its fiery dawn display, it was also my last day onboard the Royal Viking Sun. I flew home that afternoon. A couple of my good buddies met me early in the morning and we ventured out onto the breezy promenade deck. My nylon parka filled up like a sail and conversation was barely possible. Sailing under bridges is pretty awesome, hearing the dull buzz of vehicular tonnage whizzing overhead, and the sheer size of this one made the morning special. By the time the bridge has been fully repainted, the workers have to go right back to the beginning and start all over again!

Alcatraz was grimly anchored in the distance; I would have no time to visit its haunting halls. Then the city itself appeared, hilly and partially fogged in.

Alluring me, teasing me!

Alas, another time for San Fran…

What about Sydney, Australia? Was that the best sail-in? Though a spectacular morning, I do have one better. Our assistant cruise director was Australian and made a big deal out of this day. The ship had a television studio and all of the equipment was brought out so that a live broadcast could be made, the ship arriving at 5:30 AM. Sydney lies way back in a deep harbor. Suspense built slowly. The sun had not yet awoken, but barely discernable mountains hovered over us, guarding our way into the well-protected city. Suddenly, the beautiful white sails of the opera house came into view with the Sydney Harbor Bridge looming behind. Our ship conveniently docked right beside the Sydney Opera House! I went back to bed for a few more hours. I didn't have to compete with eager passengers disembarking, plus, I needed those extra z's if I was going to gad about all day.

So…

The best sail-in that I have experienced…

WITHOUT A DOUBT…

…was the first time I arrived in Rio de Janeiro, Brazil. The excitement
was palpable to all onboard, looking forward to two nights in a row
there. At 5:45 in the morning, the first thing that I noticed was the
number of hotels that loomed out of the water, with all of those
protective mountains in the background enshrouded in clouds and mist.
Then Sugar Loaf appeared, unmistakably. But where was the most
famous landmark of the city, Christ the Redeemer on Corcovado
Mountain?

Advancing bit by bit, we rounded Sugar Loaf. I looked around again
and suddenly lost my breath: there was the Redeemer, settled softly
amongst the clouds, just enough showing through the haze to create the
illusion of Christ floating! I am not religious, but couldn't help feeling a
teensy bit so that morning.

How could a sail-in get better than that? What an impression! The
statue welcomed us to the city of Rio, literally with open arms, our
introduction to a magnificent three days of samba, beautiful people, and
strolling along Copacabana Beach while sipping from coconut shells.

Ah…

Chapter 56:

THE MIDNIGHT SUN

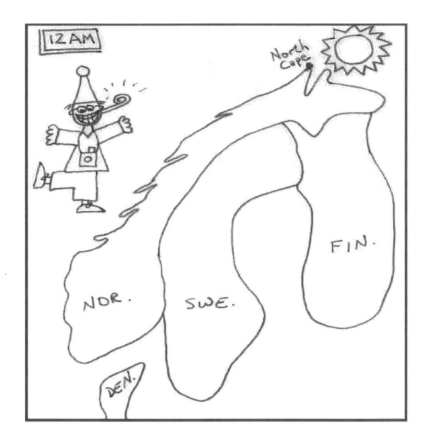

The party dispersed in the early hours of a new day, yet the sun still hovered over the horizon…

The first time I did a Baltic Cruise, we had a crew tour where we could stop and pet a reindeer, shop in a native Lapp's store, and see the traditional dress. We arrived at the North Cape, popular with tourists, looking out to the sinking sun and posing with the bronze globe sculpture there. I had already purchased the postcard picturing the sun at every hour during that time of the year when it never set, but we had to be back on our bus right before midnight! Granted, the sun was not going to set, but I wanted to be there for the Midnight Sun at midnight!

Unable to actually experience this until years later, the atmosphere was much better with fewer crowds. The daily program on the Caronia included a Midnight Sun party one evening. With iffy weather all week, the sky cleared that night in perfect fashion. Our cruise director knew how to throw a great party and went all out for this one. Goulash was served, and Norwegian glug (warm sangria!) steamed in a huge aluminum kettle. Everyone participated with a festive mood. I'm sure that every single passenger was out on the back deck that night.

We danced our hearts out to the Electric Slide, Chicken Dance, and Macarena. We ate and sipped the tangy glug. Some whales even sprayed in the distance. Could this night have gotten any better? As midnight crept closer, everyone lined up at the ship's railing with their cameras, readying for Mother Nature's quiet, but spectacular display.

Suddenly, the music stopped. The midnight hour had approached. The sun hung over the surface of the water, leaving a dull reflection, and flashes went crazy. The air was electrified, everyone posing with the Midnight Sun. The captain repositioned us so that he could take a photo up on the bridge with the sun and his clock. We all ran to the bow, thinking that we'd miss something, but soon, the ship was set back on its course.

The music continued to play for ninety minutes more. The crowd thinned, leaving only a group of die-hards. One woman danced with such abandon, such joy on her face, that it seemed as if this evening had been an emancipation of some sort for her. I felt guilty for my voyeurism, but privileged to witness this.

The festivities ended and the sun actually started to rise, disappearing up into some clouds! Outdoor appearances aside, my body informed me that bedtime had come.

Chapter 57:

STAGE MISHAPS

When I messed up onstage, I tended to mess up BIG.

The spectacle of a production show cannot be beat: sequins everywhere, legs flying, and irresistible music luring the audience to join in on the fun. The production shows I was involved in rated as the most popular evenings of the cruise. The passengers got to know us cast members throughout their weeks onboard, as if their friends or grandkids were performing for them.

After hours of rehearsing, our costume changes became a science, including where to carefully place them backstage. Zipping up a gown halfway, unsnapping a glove before the show, or precise costume order saved valuable seconds during the chaos of nine bodies scrambling to throw on their next outfits.

The lighting was programmed into the computer, our microphones tested for their appropriate levels, and the people who helped us dress, the "invisibles" doing up our Velcro and zippers, had arrived. Everyone had double-checked their fans and canes set in specific spots and the orchestra began!

BUT...

This was the live theater and something unexpected was bound to happen.

In the middle of a beach medley, we boys waited for our "Rhonda" to make her sexy entrance. Late, her zipper trouble became obvious once we saw her top flapping open all over the place onstage. Luckily, the zipper was in back, but she couldn't do any of her choreography facing upstage. I had to sit next to her and give her a kiss. That night, after just a quick peck, I did up that dastardly bit of hardware in as subtle a manner as possible for poor Rhonda. She was supposed to help ME!

I forgot to change my shoes once for a very pivotal kick line number where we all had to look like one person. Everyone wore white shoes, except me, in black.

Great.

An astute passenger noticed it, too.

Another time, I was dancing and felt something strange at my ankles. I looked down and, oh, it was my fellow cast mate, fallen into a heap on the floor. Later during that same show, dancing a Charleston piece where we had to strongly arch our backs, collapse them, and then do frantic kicks, the spaghetti strap around the neck of this poor girl snapped (right at the "strongly arch our backs" part) exposing all of her girlie bits for the audience to ogle at. The number contained a lot of arm movements and when she didn't do any of them, instead clutching onto her chest, at least her dignity remained somewhat intact.

One of the saddest things to see onstage is a dead wig. They just look so pathetic off of the head, off their foam, in a rat's nest pile on the stage. The situation becomes even worse to look over at my beautifully made-up partner and see her uselessly bobby pinned wig cap with her glitzy gown and eyelashes for days, valiantly smiling as if nothing is wrong.

The girls came on to do a number one night, mincing about and looking lovely with pink feather boas. One, two, three, four showgirl kicks, all toes pointed beautifully, when one of the feet landed perfectly into the feather loop of the girl's costume next to her.

Utter disaster!

The kicker tried to extricate her guilty foot from the feathery mess and the boa wearer, trying not to strangle herself from the ever-tightening neon pink noose, realized her need for desperate measures. She gathered all of her strength, snapped her head forward, eyes bulging seconds before her last breath, freeing the horrid foot as it landed with an audible "thwonk". The show concluded with no fatalities.

One time, the cast was all onstage singing and I got a bit too excited, lifting my arm prominently into the air and doing our spinny choreography (meant to be done sixteen counts later by everyone) too early. I looked ridiculous during my solo moment, but afforded my fellow performers a nice little chuckle. Make that a nice BIG chuckle.

In a different show, one of our guys forgot his sparkly pants, so I had to rush on and cover him. I had no idea what I was doing, so I just picked up a girl, spun her around a few times, and waved my arms elegantly. That disaster was a bit less obvious, thank goodness.

Trips and falls are a given. The ship is moving, feathers get loose, and the performing area can be slippery. On the Caronia, our "stage" was the ballroom dance floor. Wearing tap shoes on that surface was akin to ice-skating with patent-leather shoes on. Most of my falls luckily happened during rehearsal, like the time I tried to Charleston with my predecessor's unadjusted longer pants on.

Boom!

Or the time dressed as clowns and wearing huge plastic shoes that could've fit a sasquatch. At one point, from the slippery floor, I looked over and saw that two of my fellow clowns had fallen victim, too. (pun intended)

The women wore spectacular white glow-in-the-dark dresses during a waltz number that we did. The couples glided along, creating a magical atmosphere of romantic Vienna, and one unlucky girl stumbled on her formidable train, bringing her astonished partner right down on top of her, high-heel shoes tragically pounding sideways onto the unforgiving stage. They quickly untangled to continue the once beautiful formation, but the magic was over. At least the clean-up crew didn't have to mop the stage that night.

My worst fall comes in two parts.

Doing a number with another guy, we played "Madonna's" back-up boys. As I went to lift up "Madge", my Velcroed pants came undone, falling heavily, evilly to my knees. This bulk shackled me and I tried pulling them back up into their rightful position while still stupidly attempting to pick up the girl. I didn't want to mess up the choreography, see. Instead, I spread my legs for support, forgetting that the fallen pants didn't give any leeway.

Down came Madonna, on top of her silly boy, while miraculously continuing to sing through her dirty looks at me! The audience was in hysterics and my face matched the red, rebellious pants that I had by now torn off. Those babies found themselves down at the tailor's the next day, Velcro urgently replaced.

During our meet and greet after the performance with the audience, I learned that my pants had made quite the impression. One man came up to me that I had been friendly with all cruise and said he didn't recognize me. I was quite confused. Sure, I wore my glasses during the day, but he had seen all of our shows and spoken to me afterwards. I looked at him, very puzzled and he continued, "I didn't recognize you just now with your pants on."

Chapter 58:

THE FIRST ADVENTURE

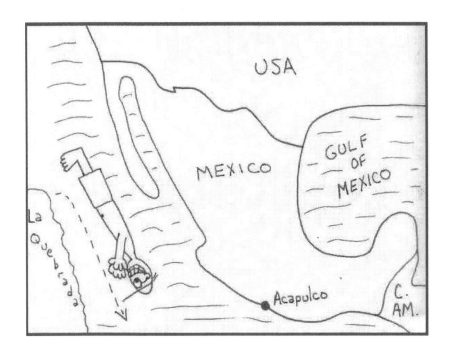

My fellow adventurer and I had just arrived and didn't want to leave.
The last diver flung himself in perfect form from the impressive waiting
area with its makeshift altar for last-minute prayers. We admired the
empty twisting concrete staircase that led down to the viewing area and
also noticed that on a little cliff to the left, there was some other diving
going on…

My cast had just boarded the old Holland America Rotterdam,
rehearsing hard and in great need of some time away. Acapulco,
Mexico lay outside as port-of-the-day. My friend's big goal was to buy
an engagement ring for her boyfriend. Finding a guide, he led us

through an overwhelming maze of markets set up right by the ship. Her wheeling and dealing settled with the choice jeweler, our journey to La Quebreda (Spanish for "broken cliff") began. The site is famous for watching the daring divers that give everyone heart attacks as they hurl themselves into what looks like a shallow wave of water surrounded by craggy rock.

We cabbed to the crowded point and caught the very last of the daring men making the one hundred and thirty-six foot jump into fifteen feet of surging ocean! The crowd applauded wildly and quickly dispersed. One of the dark aquamen posed for pictures and graciously accepted tips from his awed fans.

Novices practiced off to our left. Watching them for a bit, we noticed one of them wave and approach us, asking if we wanted to go swim with him, right in the area where the divers had just been! We couldn't believe it! Wasn't this sacred diving water? How could two gringos like us just jump into the drink normally "reserved" for THE divers?

(A side note: Was this guy really into our having an interesting visit to La Quebreda, or just lusting after my attractive mate? She was wearing a bikini, after all, a buxom blondish American babe. Or did he like ME, for that matter, in my loud Bermuda shorts? Who knows, we just trustingly followed him.)

Our enthusiastic new friend guided us down the hot slippery rocks, backtracking a few times when the "path" proved too treacherous. Eventually on a landing low enough, we jumped in and enjoyed the refreshment. Junk floated all over the water's surface, but this experience was so unique, and the surge of the ocean so fun and powerful, that we simply overlooked its non-cleanliness and stayed in the moment.

These guys would probably be "real" divers one day and here we swam and hung out with them! They'd shout, "Olas! Olas! (Waves!)" to one another when the water burst forward whereupon the boys on the mini-cliff would dive. They helped each other "train"! Between breathing, staying afloat, and strategically keeping flotsam and jetsam out of my gullet, I started yelling "Olas!" too, and the guys laughed at me, as I tried to fit in.

Later on I learned that nobody had ever died jumping off of the cliff, but the divers do lose their hair quicker than normal.

Upon reaching the ship again, my friend and I learned that our other cast mates had had big adventures, too, some parasailing over Acapulco Bay! Oh, man, did I want to do that!

Next time…

Chapter 59:

STRAWBERRIES AND SANGRIA

Don't get me wrong.

The cuisine served on the ship was fantastic. But even fillet mignon can get tiring after nine months. My status as an entertainer allowed me to eat pretty much the same food as the passengers, excluding caviar and lobster.

On the Rotterdam, I ate all of my meals in the lido, sharing breakfast and lunchtime with passengers. They went to their dining room for dinner. On the Royal Viking Sun, the cast actually dressed up every night and ate in the dining room. We had our own tables basically greeting everyone else as they entered. Dinnertime was good for our visibility onboard. In our own dining area on the Caronia, waiters-in-training served us. The food was exactly the same as what was upstairs for the guests.

On all three of my ships, the crew mess hall served the rest of the mostly Philipino or Indonesian crew, ample amounts of rice and strange smelling meats always available. We had a nice variety of food to choose from and unlike the other crewmembers, were obliged to tip our waiters. They worked very hard, their tips the least that we could do for them in exchange for the wonderful meals they constantly served.

Having said all of this, going ashore to eat was a real treat depending, of course, on the port. Food on the ship was free, but the atmosphere of the ports had to be soaked up, too. Lunch at an outdoor café was usually a part of the daily routine.

Barcelona, Spain wins as my favorite place to have a lunch out. The city is so alive with many unique sections to explore, but the Gothic District, right off of the bustling street of Las Ramblas, pulled me in every time. It was here that I tasted my first tapas, delighting in the variety of bite-sized noshes available. Chorizo, a spicy local sausage, and croquettes, little potato bites smothered in cheese, top my list.

One day on the streets of Trondheim, Norway, the most powerful smell of strawberries hit me. The wind was blowing my way, so I literally had to just follow my nose until I discovered the wonderful source of this surprising air freshener. The local market was on! Berries more ripe or fresh looking never existed before that day in Trondheim. I gave myself a stomachache eating the first pint. Then I brought a bunch into the dining room to share and put on my vanilla ice cream for dessert.

Ah!

Market ecstasy played an important part of my first visit to Helsinki, Finland, too, only this time with cherries. The fruit just exploded in my mouth with tangy ripeness. I was seven years old again with a big smile and staining juice all over my fingers. That day was capped with a Nutella crepe for my "dessert".

Speaking of feeling like a little kid, at Tivoli Gardens in Copenhagen, Denmark, my friends and I heard somebody order "candy floss".

Candy floss?

What in the world was that? To our delight, the vendor reached over and served the buyer a generous pink cloud of cotton candy! I bought some of my own right after, again eating so much that I had vowed myself off sugar forever by the end of the evening.

That didn't last long.

My friend Suzannah had never been to Pisa, so we made our way to the Livorno train station. I was thirsty and bought some water, forgetting that Italians are extremely fond of their "frizante" water. I can't stand carbonated water, so I thought I'd be brilliant and just keep shaking up my bottle to release the gas bit by painfully slow bit and make it "naturale" again. We caught the train, made our way past pretty hay stacked fields, and I was still working that stupid plastic bottle like a manic maraca player. My method was entirely fruitless and all I had to show for my idiotic efforts was a sore arm and a smug friend who told me all along that I should've just invested in a new bottle of flat water.

Hanging out with my passenger friend, Dawn, I discovered the limits of my caffeine tolerance. After Dawn and I lunched together in Southampton (during which she also ingested my plentiful amount of ship gossip), she ordered us a double cappuccino each. I am not a coffee drinker. I only sip it socially, so I had no idea what I was getting myself into. Cup number one was delicious, but the laughs kept coming as more dirt was dished, so we each got ANOTHER ONE!!! Very soon, a raging headache took over my life and by the time I had said good-bye to Dawn and gotten on the phone for family catch-up time, my hands visibly shook. I am not exaggerating. Everything in moderation, right?

While in Bodrum, Turkey, on my way from the barely-there ruins of the Mausoleum of Halicarnassus (one-seventh of the Ancient Wonders containing nothing more than column stubs now), I ran into an olive market. I had never seen so many different kinds before! They came in all shapes and sizes, but more impressively, all colors, including red! My palette was used to green and black olives only, but the rest of the rainbow was represented right before my eyes.

Speaking of olives, on one of my last days in port for that particular contract, I needed to get rid of my leftover euros in Cadiz, Spain. I held up one coin and indicated to the vendor at a market that I wanted that amount of olives. Smiling, the vendor handed me a surprisingly huge bagful! I wandered about town, munching on my green food of the gods, thinking how odd it was that everyone was wearing modern clothes in this time-forgotten place. In the distance my friend Pete sat at an outdoor café drinking sangria. He has an infectious laugh and I needed to hear it, so I walked along as if I didn't see him and stumbled into one of the empty chairs at his table.

It worked.

We lounged together for the rest of that glorious afternoon drinking our delicious (and cheap!) sangria, pigging out on my perfect olives, and watching the world go by. Life doesn't get much better than that.

Chapter 60:

NO TOURS AVAILABLE

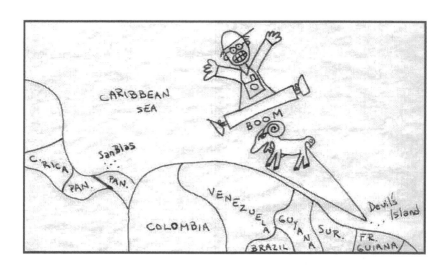

Believe it or not, some of the destinations we visited were so small that the shore excursion office had no tours to offer the passengers! There are two places that I have visited where this was the case.

It took me years to finally make it to the San Blas Islands. Tiny sprinkles of land off of the coast of Panama, I missed a chance to visit them due to Hurricane Mitch. Finally arriving on a crystal clear day, the crowded island we tendered to was unique right from the start. The Kuna Indian natives live in rudimentary shelters and hungered for our business. Many of the withered women sold their beautiful molas, colorful cloth swatches handcrafted with intricate and curvy designs, definitely worth buying. A clever man put up a primitive "Hard Rock Café" sign in front of his house. The establishment worth skipping, his idea warranted a good laugh.

My friends and I walked about in awe. This visit was like going back in time. The school was "modern", built of cinder blocks and painted nicely, but the homes had no plumbing or running water. Everybody looked healthy, but many people panhandled, too.

We hired a local man to canoe us around. If we had had more time, we could've gone over to at least one of the other closer islands. This trip did not take long, a different perspective of more primitive living and opportunity to hear our guide's commentary.

Devil's Island, off of the coast of French Guiana in South America, was another destination that we would look forward to visiting. Its name is misleading. We would actually be visiting Les Iles du Salut (the Health Islands!) and tendering to L'Ile Royale, instead of Devil's Island, which was one of another two in the whole group that we could see from Royale.

This island featured walks in the ocean breeze along the rocky, but palm tree-laden coast. A billy goat residing there butted me right in my belly when I wouldn't let it lunch on my camera case. Instead of apologizing, it casually sauntered off and ate a hibiscus.

We also spotted aguatis, little boar-like creatures with reddish coats. As we circled around the furthest coast of the easily walked isle, black monkeys made appearances within the dense jungle growth. I could have spent hours watching their antics and tried vainly to photograph some of their little faces peeking out at us from the leaves. The calls of peacocks and chickens echoed loudly throughout our walk.

Nowadays, the islands are a vacation destination and it was easy to see why. Lack of privacy was not an issue, and although nice sandy beaches were scarce, the palm trees swayed in the breeze as the ocean lapped peacefully, creating a paradise that countered the islands' dark past. A convenient refreshment stand sold water and snacks, too.

The movie "Papillion" played on the ship before our stops there. The infamous prisons depicted in the film are still available to sample. They consist of basic, small cells with thick iron bars. All of us took turns stepping in as another would chillingly slam the sturdy door shut. Mere seconds inside proved how horrible life must have been for the inmates. The intense heat of the island surrounding them while confined in their limited spaces must have been torture enough. The coast of French Guiana waited there in the distance, daring them to flee.

Unfortunately, the strong ocean currents that kept the prisoners from escaping also keep ships from visiting and on at least two occasions, my ship was unable to make its scheduled port-of-call.

Both of these island stops are little blips on the map, but interesting in their own ways. A lot of people don't like the stops where major shopping isn't available, but traveling is much more than shopping, is it not? The San Blas Islands offer exposure to a far-different culture while a stop at the lush Devil's Island area conjures feelings of gratitude to be there as a tourist.

Chapter 61:

WINTERTIME

Visiting isles loaded with palm trees and pristine beaches usually come to mind when thinking about a typical cruise. On the Caronia, however, we sailed several itineraries in December where we didn't venture far from the UK—a very cold time of year! Initially not excited about these trips, I kept an open mind and was pleasantly surprised by two towns in particular.

Honfleur, France, a town full of art galleries, contained a delightful waterfront most photogenic. I felt as if set free on a huge Hollywood soundstage designed with slightly crooked buildings cut through by narrow, cobbled streets. Wooden garage doors opened manually. A series of hillside manses featured mossy turrets. Peeping into windows,

I spied cold rooms furnished with antiques. Who lived in these ancient homes? Adding to this charm, surprisingly, was the cold weather. I desired to escape into one of these homes, warming myself up on the welcoming hearth of a stone fireplace.

Crisp air forced me to walk fast as I left town for a hillier area. A tiny church hauntingly chimed out the hours and their quarters. Workmen chipped away at decades-old plaster, attempting to refurbish the lonely structure. Heavily birded woods grew by this church; I had found my new spot! Woodpeckers pounded for their food while tits of several shapes and varieties flitted about their business, ignoring yet filling me with the joy of discovery. I had this whole area to myself and found it a frigid paradise.

During an overnight there, I ventured out with my Shore Excursion friends, Lee and Sharon, knowing that we'd be in for a wonderful dinner and French wine. Make friends with the Shorex staff! Their JOB is to know where all the goods are. Nobody from the ship was around on this cold and dark night. The passengers were nestled safely onboard, eating their dinner and watching the ship's evening entertainment.

An authentic restaurant found, we were the only ones there! I am usually "safe" and boring when I eat out, ordering chicken. But this night, that item wasn't even an option. I had to be daring. I decided on the prawns. Only a recent shrimp fan, four perfectly arranged critters came out on the plate with heads still attached! A big surprise for me, after a few deep breaths, I got a quick lesson from Sharon and was soon on my way to a delicious appetizer complemented by rich avocado.

Next came my salmon course. Those French do know how to make a sauce. A heavenly dish, I was glad that I went for it. White wine always helps, too!

What would Honfleur be like abloom with spring flowers and the resulting bees buzzing as more locals walked around? I probably wouldn't recognize the place, full of warmth and color, new charms around different corners.

I escorted two "On Your Own" tours into Bruges, Belgium. I merely counted people, greeted them as they got off of the bus in town, had two or three hours to do as I pleased, and then counted everyone again before the return trip.

Some friends and I had to take respite from outdoors and partake in what is perhaps the best hot chocolate that I have ever been privileged to drink. A steaming cup of milk was brought to our table accompanied by a hot saucer of liquid chocolate. We poured the thick darkness into the milk, stirred it up, sipped, and arrived at the pearly gates of heaven! The drink even came with sugar packets, as if more sweetener was needed! Three rich pieces of Belgian chocolate, full of buttermilk, layered onto an already amazing taste sensation.

Swans graced us on one of Bruges's many rivers and a little market sold crafts and hard candy. I witnessed a black gooey mass of liquorice being guided into a mold that pressed perfect indentations into the sugary lump. Once the candy cooled and set, a woman lifted the large piece over her marble tabletop, dropped it, and broke the confection into manageable bits, sounding like a hundred marbles hitting a wooden floor. The smell was sweet and homey.

Christmas fast approaching, several stores sold festive ornaments and nutcrackers. Many places looked welcoming, available to enter for a short spell and defrosting. I admired some detailed lace work on sale. Like Honfleur, Bruges was readily accessible by foot.

What a surprise to learn that a marble sculpture by Michelangelo, the Virgin with the Infant Jesus, made its home in town! The entrance fee to the Church of Our Lady was very reasonable: free. I had never seen any of the genius' work outside of Italy; the style of its creator was unmistakable. Mary holds her angelic baby's fat little hands, the folds of her coverings much softer than the cold marble they are carved so caringly from. Even during my second trip to Bruges, I snuck into the church to see the work again and thaw out. It is REALLY cold when churches are warmer than outside.

All over town, ivy captured stone buildings. Red maple leaves covered a distinctive turret. The sun low, it illuminated the color perfectly. By my next visit three weeks later, the leaves had fallen, but I could then appreciate the ornate pattern of the vines usurping and slowly tearing apart the circular brick structure with their minuscule tendrils. Many town bridges did not escape this invasion, either, and made for great photos, along with the step-gabled homes that I did not expect until Amsterdam.

Who knows what's to be discovered when traveling "out-of-season"? Treasures are found everywhere at all times of the year with open eyes and minds. It just depends on whether one wants to be with hundreds more tourists or not.

I met my group at a central square in Bruges just as the stores began to switch on their Christmas lights for the evening. Our warm bus opened up and a light snow began to fall.

Perfect.

Chapter 62:

CELEBRITY DISH

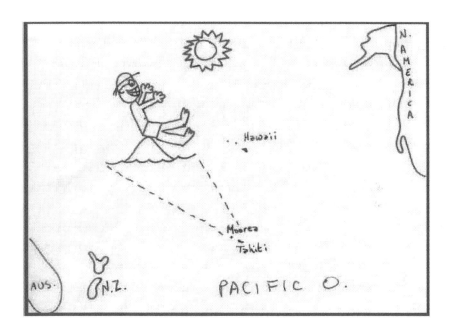

I sailed with a few celebrities. Most were very generous with their support of our performances and individual talents.

Lucie Arnaz came onboard, sang a fantastic show (never once mentioning her MOTHER during her fascinating growing-up-in-Hollywood patter!), and then indulged our request to pose for a photo. At the last second, she grabbed my chest!

HELLO!! LUCILLE BALL'S BLOOD IS FONDLING ME!!!

Then I ran into Rue McClanahan while crossing over to the other side of stage during one of my shows. "Dear Blanche", I wanted to ask, "Why aren't you watching us?" She shyly smiled at me in what I interpreted as flirtation and made me blush. After all, I was wearing a sailor suit.

Before our last cruise on the Rotterdam, my friends and I were excited to learn that it would be star-studded, including Jack Klugman and Shirley Jones. Both gave informative lectures on their careers. Mr. Klugman talked very openly about his throat cancer and how despite the sound of his voice, he was in no pain when he spoke. He approached a couple of us as we disembarked for our last time and paid us some wonderful compliments. They meant a lot coming from him, an extraordinary veteran of stage and screen.

Ms. Jones was charming, too, singing everything we had hoped for and letting us photograph her. "Oklahoma" was screened in the movie theater while she was onboard and I just HAD to watch it, knowing I was doing so with its star onboard.

Our day in Papeete, Tahiti was our last onboard the Rotterdam. Not flying until the wee morning hours, a half-day was ours to relax at the luxurious Beachcomber Parkroyal Resort.

Royalty indeed!

An exotic basket of local fruits waited for us in our rooms, most of which I had never heard of! Walking the grounds after dropping our luggage off, we ran into a groundskeeper who let us sample some fresh, slimy coconut. The pure white and gelatinous meat was different and divine.

Right at the edge of the vast South Pacific, our swimming area was an illusion pool. Mysterious Moorea tempted us off in the distance as the surf lapped musically all day. In the pool, we could swim right up to the bar, the barstools themselves resting underwater. We spent the whole day there, making up for a summer spent in Alaska. Birds snitched bar food as we savored our last moments of utter relaxation before returning to reality.

The huts built all along this resort had thatched roofs, each angled privately towards the ocean. While swimming, I looked over to one of the restaurant areas, and there sat Shirley Jones. How fun that we both enjoyed this glorious place at the same time!

My mother had clipped an article out of the paper for me about Ms. Jones. She was going through a separation from her husband. I wondered if she had been dreading what was facing her once she left our haven in paradise.

Strangely enough, I met Ms. Jones again four years later on another ship. Of course she didn't remember me, but it was fun to chat with her a bit as if we were old pals.

On the other end of the spectrum was Debbie Reynolds. She did put on a fun and interesting show, joking about being Princess Leia's mother and such. But is that what I remember most about her?

No.

She demanded unavailable caviar from a harried cocktail waiter and then had one of her people shoo us away from our viewing area on deck during sailaway. She couldn't see and wouldn't move to another seat herself.

Royalty indeed.

Chapter 63:

SHUFFLE HOP STEP

"Mike, would you be willing to teach a tap class?"

Some passengers had requested such, but our cruise director specialized in ballroom dancing; he needed "outside" reinforcements. I had previously taught dance only very casually. I accepted the challenge, but trepidation filled me.

What would they want to learn?

Would I be able to explain properly?

WOULD ANYBODY SHOW UP TO MY CLASS???

Everyone who came that first day was very enthusiastic. Despite the
different dance levels of passengers attending, they all supported one
another and I realized that day the power that any teacher has in
dispensing information. My audience was completely rapt. I got a kick
out of seeing a stage full of people old enough to be my parents or
grandparents looking to me for information.

We started with the basics: shuffles and shuffle steps. (I later learned to
avoid hopping and jumping. Beginners just don't like to leave the safe
floor. Who can blame them?) Next we circled the floor with flaps and
ball changes. A fun class, with some nice exercise, I felt like a genuine
teacher! The time flew by, too! My worries melted.

During the South America cruise, containing loads of sea days, the real
tapping began. Again, the passengers had requested the class and this
time, our dance captain from the shows helped me out. She was great
for breaking down the steps, plus, we found it necessary to teach at two
different speeds. A great choreographer, she came up with the idea of
having our tappers perform in the passenger talent show at the end of
the cruise, an idea that most of them embraced, faithfully meeting us on
every single sea day. How entertaining to observe all these women
tapping their hearts out wearing hard-soled sandals, or even the bold
ones who braved heels! And instead of tights and leotards, these dames
wore their pastel and glittery best.

Once again faced with people of many different levels, we met the
challenge by placing those less confident in the back rows of the dance
formation. This worked out just fine. Our talent ran the gamut from the
flamboyant woman who always wanted to be in front to the Italian
woman and her mother, who could barely speak English. I would

explain how to do a shuffle, "Your foot brushes front, and then brushes back", and the daughter would then translate it for her mother, who smiled and nodded in recognition, a sweet exchange to witness.

Then there was the woman who thought that she was so much worse than she was, a regular drama queen. I guess that was somewhat appropriate amongst us "theatricals", but I was amazed to see her beat herself up so much when all she had to do was just stop and think for a minute and then try again as most of the others did.

And I can't forget our few brave guys. One was quite jolly, with a white beard and cheery face. A couple of the men truly did have two left feet, but instead of giving up, they plugged on and gave tap a shot. They had lots of fun and with all of our practice time, they magically improved, bit by bit.

One woman told me that I reminded her of her son. Our youngest attendee was a singer from London's West End, a pro who had great energy for everyone else to aspire to. A former opera singer joined us (who performed double duty with an aria in the talent show, too) and, last but not least, there was a sweet blue-eyed woman who was a natural (she had brought heeled character tap shoes, standard wear for a professional!) Having obviously danced before, she performed with charming facial expressions and had a blast on that stage.

The time to start discussing "costumes" came. Our routine was choreographed and all that we had to do was continue polishing the number. There was all sorts of brouhaha over what should've been worn and why. I kept out of it, but heard these women debating and deciding, as if back in high school discussing the importance of the perfect prom dress!

Decisions, SUCH DECISIONS!!!!

The big day of the show arrived and hype for "The Tapping Cuties" was big. I had requested that we close the show, and our cruise director was only too happy to comply. I couldn't believe how nervous I was, fully invested emotionally by this time! They had truly become MY kids and I had to calm some of their jittery nerves, too.

After our grand introduction, they made their chipper, overly rehearsed entrances to much applause; the music began…

They were great! The number flew by, ending with a magnificent kick line. Intentional, we knew that the audience would eat the line right up and they did! Stars were born that day! I so enjoyed the looks of pride (relief?) on their faces when our bit finished.

Right after the performance, the assistant cruise director, who emceed the show, told us all to stay onstage. It happened to be my birthday and he led everyone into a six-hundred-member rendition of the big song. What a surprise! The ballroom had been packed for the talent show and I'd never heard that many people sing to me before.

By this point, I was practically choking back tears. I will always cherish that moment. I gave all of my ladies kisses (with nice firm handshakes for the boys!), everyone basking in the glorious limelight of a job well done.

Chapter 64:

PORTUGAL

Who knew that with numerous visits I would become better acquainted with Lisbon, Portugal than my own hometown of Rochester, NY? It is strange, but true.

My first visit to Portugal was in Leixos where we shuttled into rainy Porto. Touring the Avaleda vineyard in the wine country that day, I saw delicious Vinho Verde being poured into bottles, all lined up like green guards, pasted with their quaint labels, and boxed, ready to be shipped all over the world. The whole process fascinated me with its efficiency. I have since fallen in love with that particular wine.

Once in the actual town of Porto, the cathedral rested up on an imposing square draped in fog, adding to its allure for me. Despite the dreary day, I was surprised to enter and see the stained glass shining in its colorful glory. I guess any light will do the job. The view outside, from where the giant Romanesque structure stood, provided an unobstructed look down into the old town, seemingly drawn for a stage backdrop in forced perspective, the angles of the streets and buildings that extreme. A boy played with his little black dog in the rain and I noted how much grittier this town was than anything we had just seen further north in Scandinavia.

Rain showers continued on with me and I sheltered myself inside many different buildings. Beautiful blue and white tiles were incorporated everywhere! I sloshed my way across town to see the iron bridge designed by Mr. Eiffel via several wineries, all offering inviting and dry spaces underground to sample their fine wares. My mind was already occupied with Vinho Verde, though.

From Lisbon, a jeep tour took a daring group of us off-road into forests inhabited by trees thick with moss. At the westernmost point of Europe (Cabo de Roca), the vicious winds nearly blew me off the steep cliff that we had gingerly stepped onto for photos and views of the ferocious ocean.

The day in Portugal that most impressed me, though, is the one that I had from my first visit to Lisbon. I made a "pilgrimage" to Fatima, an important destination for devout Catholics. I was curious about the history behind the original sightings of the Virgin Mary allegedly occurring there.

In 1917, three peasant children from the area "saw" the Virgin. A shrine was built on the location and the town exploded with pilgrims and miracle seekers. I was shocked to come across wax effigies available for purchase of pretty much any ailing body part. If I had a sore leg, for example, I could buy a wax leg and throw it into a ceremonial fire. If I were devout enough, my leg would be healed!

I was absolutely flabbergasted when I saw the path that the very devout traveled in order to prove their humility. A huge cathedral stood at the bottom of a long declining square. An intimidating amount of carpeting led to its doors on which people crawled all the way down on their KNEES! I cringed to see an elderly woman in this process, crying and suffering her way to the end, utterly floored that she would put herself through what must have been extremely painful. She kept at it, though, satisfying her own beliefs.

I felt like I did not belong in Fatima, much the way that I feel in any cathedral. I appreciate the architecture and the history of these places as a tourist and marvel at the sense of smallness that I experience in these grand buildings, but I do not understand the customs. I am invading millions of private prayers.

It was only later in the season that I finally met the actual city of Lisbon and I have since enjoyed its hilly streets many more times. Hiking up to the fortress of Castelo São Jorge, winding and losing my way through the byways of the Alfama district, I am rewarded with a view of the whole city. One night a bunch of friends and I dined at a restaurant featuring fado. We enjoyed first-hand the guttural pinings of the singers, who belted out powerful and emotional tunes, but sounded as if they'd never had a voice lesson in their lives. Their music was primitive and real.

The waterfront area where we ported had recently developed an extensive strip of restaurants and outdoor establishments. For whatever reason, Lisbon was usually a late sail. Most crew took advantage of a nice dinner out, looking over to the statue of Christ matching the one in Rio, and the long bridge connecting Lisbon to the beach area, designed exactly like San Francisco's Golden Gate.

Lights shone brilliantly on the statue and bridge. Our ship had just sounded the half hour until we all had to be back. By the time the bills were paid and the last bits of beverage consumed, a rush of crew now struggled to get back to the gangway on time. One half hour later, we slowly set sail and floated out under the bridge, through the long harbor, and onto wherever awaited next, full of fun memories from another great time in Portugal.

Chapter 65:

SWIMMING WITH THE TURTLES

Barbados, named after the bearded fig tree ("barba" is Spanish for "beard"), is the Caribbean island that I always leave loving more. It offers a huge array of things to do, the people are friendly, and the land has a rich history.

For one month on the Caronia, a troupe of wonderful Brits performed onboard who all had experience on London's West End, the American equivalent of Broadway. A fun group, I enjoyed getting to know these people closer to my age. They also proved to me that no matter where from, we theater people are all the same: young at heart and goofy. I hung out with them on an all-day trip in Barbados to swim with turtles, one of the best things I've ever done in the natural world.

Our day started with a brief tour around the island, admiring the flora, sampling sugar cane, and stopping to take pictures at scenic panoramas, which included a former sugar mill looking very much like a wind mill. At one point, we also came across free samples of rum punch, a nice bonus on this sultry day. Nearby, a few years previously on a rainy day, I did a double take after seeing a couple of zebras grazing in a field! It seems that they had since disappeared.

At a little beach resort, we hired out a boat and settled in for our mini trip down the coast. The clear sky, green palms, and delicious-looking sapphire water enticed. We had not a care in the world upon the calm ocean. Arriving at the turtles' area, masked and snorkeled, we jumped in to enjoy a surprising sea ballet. The green sea turtles swam close by with their beautifully patterned shells, lured over to us with frozen fish. Other colorful fish (alive!) joined us and I witnessed one meet its untimely death between the fierce jaws of a turtle that apparently craved more than the icy offerings.

These gentle creatures moved gracefully, so differently than I had imagined, having seen them only lumber around on land before this day. I touched their smooth curvy shells and admired their comfort down in this blue aquatic territory where I was so dependent on the nearby surface for its safety and air. I have always felt content in this environment, free to float surrounded by warm water and muffled silence.

I could have spent all day getting to know these guys better and feeling more the privilege of their company. However, our stomachs started to grumble, triggered no doubt by all of those appetizing fish guts.

Comfortably ashore, I ordered coleslaw prepared with raisins and curry, a delicious mix. Some curious monkeys entertained us, peeking down from their boreal perches with almost too-human faces. They waited for handouts that we knew better than to give.

As we arrived back to the port, I reached into the back seat of our hired van and retrieved a long piece of sugar cane that our guide had given me. I had only requested a little sample for everyone to try, but he had given me a whole stalk! What was I going to do with it? I passed it off to one of the local women hanging around with her girlfriends in the terminal. You would have thought I'd given her fifty dollars from the gratitude she expressed!

It was the least I could do, ma'am. Thanks for sharing with us your wonderful island.

Chapter 66:

REINCARNATION

I know that I have lived in Florence, Italy. It must have been another lifetime. From the moment I first arrived at the city on a solo trip, to all of the subsequent visits while escorting ship tours, I just KNOW that I have walked those streets before and taken in all of that exquisite art and architecture.

More specifically, I believe that I was one of Michelangelo's aides or students, having always felt a deep connection to the works of this literal Renaissance man. It is a feeling more of just "appreciation". Did I perhaps polish those sensuous marble curves of flesh and muscle or mix his paint? Was I one of his models even? I feel like I was important in his life, yet it's the city itself that speaks to me. I don't feel this strongly about anywhere else in Europe.

So far…

I take to the streets calmly in Florence, like I'm home. I am a tourist everywhere I go, but something different happens to me in this city, like a remembering, rather than a discovery. This is especially true in the piazza off of the main square at the Medici Palace, the piazza that the Uffizi overlooks, containing the sculpture promenade of the great artists. How much time did I spend there in my former life?

And David. Mighty David. Was I in love with this statue? I am unable to turn away from its sheer size and artistry, representing such beauty. In the Accademia Museum, I know that it's coming, yet I turn around the corner, see the god-like perfection glowing at the end of the hall, and have to catch my breath. I was THERE when David was first unveiled. I had to be.

Why are we attracted to certain things so strongly? I wasn't particularly exposed to Michelangelo's work when I was a child, but I remember my mother telling me how she had seen the Pieta in Rome a few days before a maniac attacked it with a sledgehammer. I didn't even know that Florence was a cultural high point until a wise friend strongly advised me to stop by for a few days during previous travels. I can't believe that I would have otherwise passed the city by!

I got off the train from Venice, walked around the streets for a bit and within hours knew that the city was mine. I had returned.

Chapter 67:

MG, PHONE HOME

"Hello, Gram?" (as if I didn't know who it was…)

"Michael?! Where are you THIS time?" (truly a valid question…)

I tried to call home at least once every other week, but it was always tough keeping in touch. I was sailing on an older ship that did not have satellite access from my cabin. Not only did I have to wait until late afternoon on a port day to call due to the six hour time change (which was also about when I'd have to reboard the ship), but I had to actually first FIND a phone not occupied by a crew member talking for the entire duration of his or her limited port time.

The international sign for a phone card (this doesn't apply in Spain if you know the phrase "tarjeta para telefono") is to hold out your thumb and pinkie to your face. If the vendor still looked bewildered, or thought I was asking for an actual phone, I'd make a little air square and insert "it" into an air phone. That would then be the cue to give me directions in the native tongue (in some cases, it really was Greek to me) to go to yet another vendor on "blah blah blippety-blah" street.

What, then, dear God/Allah/Buddha, if I didn't have any local currency? Find a bank, hope it's open and willing to exchange American money for the local dough, and repeat the trip to the bemused vendor. I used to have about ten envelopes labeled one each with French francs, Italian lira, Spanish pesetas, Swedish, Norwegian, Icelandic, and Danish kroners, Estonian krooni, British pounds, and German deutschemarks, etc, etc, etc…

HALLELUJAH EURO!!!

I called home once from the midst of the Amazon River basin (literally the middle of nowhere) on a phone that I initially had little faith in. Sitting there in the hot sun with a faded blue bubble around it, the phone not only miraculously worked, but I had a remarkably clear line home. Everyone said that I sounded like I was next door.

Not quite.

Was all of this travel worth the frustration I'd feel when I'd procure a phone, but it didn't work? When my card couldn't function in that country? When I never figured out how to get to the English -menu? When I'd finally get through, only to be leaving a homesick message on an answering machine?

My answer is a resounding "Absolutely!"

Chapter 68:

SOME NATIVES

I found the original Spice Girl!

I have met a countless number of people on my travels: guides, dispatchers, vendors, etc. Two in the Caribbean particularly stand out because they were so colorful and friendly (attempting to sell me something, yes!)

In Grenada, my friends and I hired a guy for a look-see around the beautiful and lush spice island, learning all about mace coming from nutmeg, sampling the bark from which cinnamon comes, and savoring cocoa ground right into our hands, such a luscious and rich aroma!

Taken to a little shack on the side of a road, we met Louina, who ran the place. A more shriveled and small woman could not be found, but she lit up like Times Square as we walked in. I was immediately taken with her personality and enthusiasm. She wore a red shirt with colorful trim, fitting in with the local style, but then had on a horrid black baseball cap advertising a popular sports brand.

It jars the senses to see such modern accoutrement. Imagine being on the plains of Africa, for instance. Touring a Masai village, the shaved headed inhabitants wrapped with bright red blankets that stand out so sharply from the arid, brown land are reciting their ancient chants and spreading dung onto their shelters. Looking closer, one of them is wearing a watch!

AGH!!!!!!

Louina modeled her goofy cap proudly and I bought a lot from her, so I figured that it was OK for me to take her picture. I called her the original "Spice Girl" and she laughed very loudly. Did she get my joke, or was she just trying to flatter me?

I bet it was the latter.

From the souvenir shack to Annandale Falls, we admired women balancing baskets of fruit on their heads and got talked into buying a few spice necklaces, perfectly fragrant for our little cabins. Arriving back into town, I saw that the same calabash full of the spices that I had bought from my girl Louina sold for HALF the price I'd paid! Scam Spice ripped me off!

A couple years later, I found myself in Dominica. Unable to port at the town of Rousseau, we ported clear across the other side of the island where nothing (literally) existed. The passengers had to rent cabs and satisfy their shopping fixes faraway in town, but we crew stayed in the area and explored on our own.

I set up our tour for the day. Boat drill scheduled in the morning, I wanted to reserve a driver early so that we would not be left behind. A whole load of guys lined the gangway, ready to rent out their boats and services for the day. Three of them started to fight over me, but I went with Lawrence. After all, he had the best price!

One of the other guys caught my attention. Very slim, animated, and sporting thin dreadlocks, he was unique amongst everybody else, especially with his name: Spaghetti. I laughed out loud and almost regretted not hiring him just because he would have been such fun. During drill, I looked down from the verandah deck and gave Lawrence a "thumbs up". He was still waiting for us.

Our driver, jokingly calling himself Lawrence of "Areebia", brought us into the Indian River, one of the supposed three hundred and sixty-five that Dominica has to offer. We sailed by a rusty wreck, half submerged and on its side, that met its untimely end during Hurricane Marilyn. Lawrence showed us native flowers, pointed out termites' nests, and caused quite a stir at one point when warning us not to put our temperature testing hands into the inviting water due to ALLIGATORS!

His joke.

We passed a strangler fig that had fallen to the ground in a hollow cylindrical shape: that which it had strangled had long since died and rotted away, making for a beautiful end product. The trees hung thickly over us, creating a natural tunnel of shade. The aboveground roots of the dense mangrove area we next entered were a million slithering snakes, frozen. I found a little turtle poking out for some air, only to deflate a few moments later with the announcement that, indeed, my turtle was a coconut.

Ending up at a wonderful bar in the middle of the jungle, we could lie in hammocks and relax all afternoon. The strong passion fruit rum punch flowed.

Suddenly, the rains came. We were not the only ones there, by a long shot. Many people from our ship had come to this place, and with the advent of the stormy skies, crammed into this now cluttered space waiting for the showers to subside. Spaghetti and his group among us, everyone got to know him well.

Back out of the river again, the Purple Turtle Café provided delicious food. My favorite Caribbean fare, plantains, was unavailable, but I settled for some chicken fajitas. The breeze was blowing, the strong sun shone again, and Spaghetti had found a girlfriend.

He was entitled to a perfect day, too.

Chapter 69:

ABBA

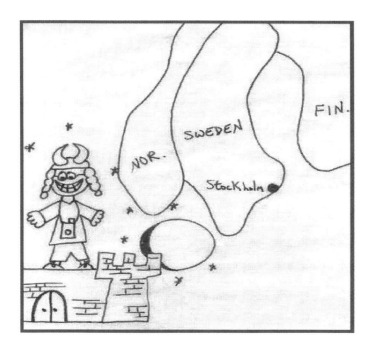

I always dreaded the day that I would feel "old".

One of the first times this happened was in Stockholm, Sweden, when my friend Suzannah and I discovered with much surprise and excitement that the Nordik Museum featured an exhibition of ABBA memorabilia. We oohed and aahed over the gaudy costumes and gold albums for at least a half hour, but were startled when one of our younger peers turned to us innocently and asked, "Who ARE these guys?"

Suzannah and I just looked at each other agape, knowing that there was no hope in bringing our cultural protégé up to speed. She was a true Eighties Girl. Scary.

Stockholm contains many parks and the entire city is built on several islands, so we were left with a lovely impression of the water-filled scene. Eventually, we found ourselves at the fascinating Wasa Museum; a sunken ship had been dug out of the mud in the deep harbor, which resulted in its being fully preserved even after hundreds of years. The poor top-heavy vessel set sail, immediately foundered and sank. Luckily for us, the water it rested in was frigid and bacteria-free, preserving the wood perfectly.

In the evening, we took part in a festival where an ABBA imitation band played. We stopped and sang our little hearts out, the best we could do in place of the defunct quartet themselves. Our young mate STILL had no idea who they were and actually appeared bored!

Being June, the sky remained quite light. I walked the streets of Stockholm until arriving in the oldest part of town, a Medieval-like island where all of the thin streets kept me on a straight and fascinated course.

Docked and quiet for the night, the tourist Viking ship with its strong and curved masthead struck a formidable silhouette. I strolled by the palace where earlier, I had caught the changing of the guard. A near-full orange moon hung off of a turret and I wondered how a king and queen slept. The cobbles under my feet echoed hollowly as I passed under dark windows and crept by slinking, shadowed cats. Deep, resonant chimes knolled out each quarter hour.

The sky lightened as I crossed over to the city's nature park. The grass sparkled with a new coating of dew when I passed a statue of Jenny Lind, ("Ah, yes! P. T. Barnum's "Swedish Nightingale!") and spooked a young deer resting nearby. Deer in the middle of a city!

The sun rose that morning at 3:48 and I returned to the ship at 4:50. Stockholm woke up as I readied for bed, the music of ABBA my lullaby.

Chapter 70:

THE COTE D'AZUR

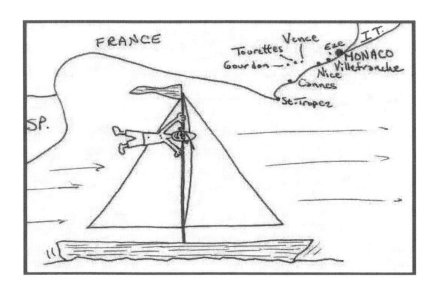

My first impression of the French Riviera was not the numerous yachts that floated about, harboring the ultra-wealthy, not the pastel movie-set homes that must have had hundreds of stories to tell, and not the beaches, quite scrawny compared to those I'd seen in Spain. My first impression of the French Riviera was the gorgeous magenta color splashed onto all of the stonework enclosing the train station provided by the bright bougainvillea.

These gorgeous flowers grew everywhere in the Mediterranean, but for some reason, they burned into my brain when I first tendered into the quaint Villefranche del Mar, nestled right into the mountains so near to the sea. Three levels of roads, "corniches", could be chosen from to traverse the Riviera. The bougainvillea provided a vibrant contrast to the dull stone that they clung to.

Villefranche was an excellent place for us to be based. From there, I escorted a tour to St. Paul de Vence, a magnificent medieval town that still harbored many artists. The town, paved with patterned cobblestones, contained squares with burbling fountains decorated quaintly with fresh flowers and vines. An olive tree laden with small, unripe fruit caught my eye. This town was one of several that perched on top of a peak, offering a stunning view into the valley towards the sea. We traveled for what felt like hours, climbing and climbing to get to our destination, and our guide told us that we were no more than ten miles from the water, the Alps off in the distance!

Eze was another one of these enclaves that looked as if it would fall off of its dizzying platform, along with Tourettes and Gourdon. We passed so many more, that weeks would be needed to visit them all. Many of the villages had been abandoned! The road up to visit one of these towns was a mass of twisty curves, with overhanging rocks threatening to collapse at any time. On my trip to Gourdon, our driver broke his personal record of perfection by driving just a tiny bit too close to the edge of the road, busting out a huge bus window on the right side. This event made for an unexpectedly exciting morning, despite our driver's being humbled in front of thirty-odd anxious tourists.

The train system in this area of the world was excellent and many other towns thus easily accessible. Cosmopolitan Nice provided museums and enormous flower markets that the smaller towns lacked. The prevalent wrought iron railings surrounding the buildings' balconies reminded me of New Orleans' origins. I walked from Villefranche to Nice once. The views of Nice's large and sparkling harbor as I ascended onto the other side of the mountain were worth my sore feet.

Tina Turner and Elton John own homes that overlook Nice and it was always my secret unfulfilled hope that I'd run into one of them at a tiny store. I would then be invited up for a bit of a chat and perhaps a dip in their luxurious in-ground pools while savoring peeled grapes and baguettes.

One day, after my friend Suzannah and I had both escorted, she asked me what I was going to do with my afternoon. I saw her eyes light up as she asked if I wanted to venture with her to Monaco! Only a short train ride away, we took that trip easily and walked the palace grounds, peeking into the cathedral holding Princess Grace's grave. Our whirlwind trip to the mega-wealthy city had fulfilled our daily dose of adventure.

Later, the day after the Grand Prix, I happened to be on a scenic tour of Monaco. The racetrack consisted of the city's actual roads! Monaco was crowded and compact enough, but to set up this complex racetrack and bleachers, to bar all of the traffic, must have been a logistical nightmare.

Our bus was stuck in traffic, and our funny guide commented that soon we would be at the starting position for the race! We crept up a bit more, closer to the line.

Crept... Closer...

Crept... Closer...

Finally, at pole position, our guide broke into a manic commentating frenzy as if we sped hundreds of miles an hour instead of inches per minute.

Nobody was left in the stands to cheer for us.

I was in Cannes one year on the day that the film festival opened. Unfortunately, we had to leave by the time the stars would be arriving. The energy there was intense, though, everyone abuzz, the theaters displaying building-sized movie ads of the most popular films that season. Miles of red carpets spread out and red stanchions kept separate the soon-to-appear glitterati from everymen like me.

St. Tropez was the one stop in the Cote d'Azur that knocked me over. Artists sat along the harbor area selling their gorgeous works overlooking enormous sailboats and very white yachts that shone until blinding. The water mesmerized me as it reflected off of their bows, nature's kaleidoscope of ever-changing patterns.

Everything in St. Tropez was the crème de la crème. I felt so out of place. A few people had seen celebrities that night. I personally looked for drag queens. Having done the musical "La Cage Aux Folles" a couple of times, which takes place in St. Tropez, I just couldn't leave the town satisfied until I'd seen my stage counterparts in their true milieu. I was not disappointed as three giggling wo/men rounded a corner as I returned to the ship tenders.

Back in Villefranche, I lounge at an outdoor café with my cast. I have just ordered a tasty ham galette (a crepe made of wheat) and the sun is setting. The white wine is delicious and the laughs are plenty. I am spying on a couple luxuriously dining out on their balcony. Their neighbors still have laundry hanging out in the slight breeze that has just come up. My pals and I can look out onto the Mediterranean and see our little ship waiting for us to tender back to it.

But none of us want to.

Chapter 71:

"SORRY, WE'RE OPEN"

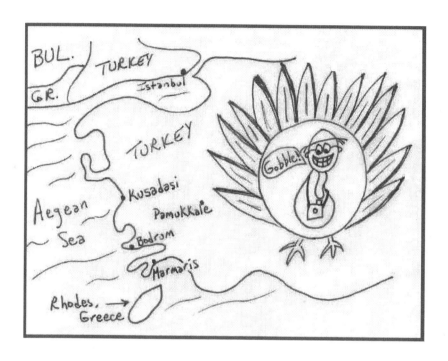

Any seasoned traveler has certainly come across his or her share of hilarious translations into English such as the one above, a sign I enjoyed at a little shop in Istanbul, Turkey. This day also featured a serendipitous stumbling upon a huge book market, the biggest I have ever seen anyplace, where old maps labeled "Constantinople" could be purchased. It's interesting how obsolete items can become somebody's treasure.

Pete the Printer and I took a side trip from Kusadasi one day to Pamukkale, home of Turkey's "Cotton Castle" where visitors can enjoy the surreal calcium deposits that over the years have created an enormous tumor-like mountain sparkling like fresh snow and resembling a huge frosted mini-wheat. It looked as if we should have been skiing there, but instead wore shorts on a brutally hot day. Some of the deposits, dripping infinitesimally slowly, created salt-looking icicles. A few rebellious Turks sported bikinis and bathed in the little pools formed within the structure. Strictly a no-no, I saw the sign: "Entering the travertines is not certainly allowed to protect this amazing natural beauty as it used to be."

Bodrum, Turkey featured a fantastic underwater archeological museum. I luckily stayed behind with one of the slower passengers that I had escorted and learned that she had been a diver and done a lot of archeological work herself! She happily shared her fascinating stories and information with me. I asked her with some trepidation if she had seen signs of pollution underwater, even in her heyday decades ago. Her answer was an unfortunate, "yes", adding that I would not believe how polluted the oceans are. She had seen proof everyday.

On a better note, we observed algae-coated elephant tusks and hippo teeth that had been excavated from a wreck sinking centuries ago. Glass beads from ancient Greek ships had become fossilized, actually turning into stone! Tin and glass ingots in amphorae had melted together into incoherent messes. My new friend took me out to lunch that afternoon. I think she appreciated her attentive audience of one, enrapt with her knowledge and adventures. We passed by a market selling "genuine fake" watches.

After the frenzy of Istanbul and Bodrum, Marmaris surprised us--a resort town! Lined with palm trees, the streets looked imported from Los Angeles. Many nice boats harbored in the attractive marina that we passed in order to get into the center. Miles of beaches covered with sunbathers spread along the main road filled with restaurants and stores selling the ubiquitous Turkish Delight. Kiosks sprouted up through red and white beach umbrellas, too. One welcomed us with a sign, "You can just drinks".

That was the place we chose.

Chapter 72:

BARTHELONA

This, of course, is Barcelona, Spain. Despite my previous six years of studying Spanish, I had forgotten about the lisp incorporated into this region's way of speaking until visiting for the first time.

Suzannah and I whirled off on another one of our ambitious trips. Just how much could we see of a major European city in eight hours? We literally jumped ship as soon as clearance was granted. Barely 7:30 AM, we sped off before any passengers, still eating breakfast! Suzannah had been to the city before and enthusiastically briefed me the whole previous week about Barcelona's glory and all that we would have to fit into our speedy day.

Coursing through the extensive dockyard, we realized that we could not have ported any further away from town. Hearts pounding, we finally stumbled into the city proper and a subway that we immediately boarded. Climbing stairs and trucking through numerous streets, we still had quite a way to the Parc Guell. When we got there, it was closed! Our overly anxious selves had arrived before 9:00 AM! Loud parrots in the palms were just waking up, laughing at us and mocking our enthusiasm.

Suzannah had already turned me on to Antoni Gaudi and his wonderful architecture with the passion in which she spoke of him. I peeked at my first tastes from behind the heavy iron gate so efficiently keeping us out of the park. Once in, we raided the place like barbarians. So much ahead of his time, Gaudi broke tradition and created fully what he envisioned in his brilliant mind. His designs twist and drip with fanciful color, sometimes using broken tiles as mosaics. His are childlike visions, reminiscent of Dr. Suess. The park's background is a series of columns able to be woven in and out of, underneath a plaza with walls that snake around decorated with tons more tiles. From here, the scope of the grounds can be appreciated. A fantasyland, this park long preceded anything from Mr. Disney.

Next on our list: the Sagrada Famiglia, Gaudi's grand cathedral, far from being completed. Construction started in 1882 and if work progresses regularly, it MAY be finished in my lifetime! My eyes widened as we approached the huge sand castle, living up to Suzannah's hype. Gaudi created fantastic shapes sprinkled with Biblical figures from cold, hard stone. That day, Suzannah admirably conquering her fear of heights, we climbed up into one of the lofty turrets comprising the cathedral and saw workers actually assembling one of the fruit-like adornments that are the icing on the east side of the structure. Huge columns lay in pieces off in a side yard. Someday they would be added to the complex puzzle. I could not believe that the Sagrada Famiglia was being built right before my eyes!

Flitting about the city, we hunted down two other of Gaudi's buildings, Casas Batllo and Mila, one under scaffolding. This led us to Las Ramblas, the unique thoroughfare lined with endless newspaper and pet vendors, cafes, and most interestingly, street performers. Las Ramblas is a free circus; each "act" has made itself unique. Most are mime-types sporting incredibly creative costumes: the bronze-looking cowboy, the fiery tree women, and the clever man who gels his long hair back, wears a stiff coat, holds onto a lamppost and looks as if he's in the middle of a hurricane! Put a little bit of money in their boxes, and the acts "turn on" for you!

By the time Suzannah and I turned onto Las Ramblas, we realized that we hadn't eaten all day, but didn't want to take up the time to eat big. A fast food ice cream cone had to do. The señorita handed me my cone, in a paper lining, and I hungrily squeezed it so hard that the thing popped right out. My errant cone shot up like a 1992 Summer Olympic diver, arched horrifically, and promptly crashed ice cream-first onto the tiled floor via Suzannah's once-fresh shirt. I was a little boy again and wanted to cry. My ice cream was dead! Luckily for me though, both Suzannah, hysterical, and the señorita, generous, witnessed the incident. I cleaned up the gooey mess and chowed down my replacement right away.

The Gothic Barrio lies right off of Las Ramblas. In this medieval section of Barcelona, where COLUMBUS had been, the architecture is so time-locked that one leaves the neighborhood with a sore neck from all of the craning. The cathedral contains a rose window to rival any others in the world.

On one occasion, Suzannah, Pete the Printer, and I ordered tapas at an outdoor café. A woman wandered by, a giant bumblebee displaying her yellow dress trimmed with black froufrou. Obviously a street performer, she also carted along a woman (her mother?) in a wheelchair! Despite my best attempts, I could not take my eyes off of this outrageous figure. The second we made eye contact, I had inadvertently "invited" her to perform for us with music from her silly looking boombox.

Suzannah, completely exasperated with me for getting into such situations, gave me a grim look because now we had to scramble around and give this castanet-bearing character some money. Dancing around us a bit, totally invading personal space, and a mediocre singer, at best, she became an unforgettable part of our adventures in this diverse city.

One of my best discoveries in Barcelona, I was again traversing Las Ramblas and saw an advertisement for an art exhibit by Yann Arthus-Bertrand. He made his name by photographing the "Earth From the Air". I had seen his work only on postcards and was thrilled to learn that a fuller exhibit was on display right here in the city. What luck! The show (held in rooms misted with aromatic ambience) included pictures from the Blue Lagoon in Iceland, the monasteries of Meteora in Greece, and the fallen columns found in Pamukkale, Turkey, places that we had just visited while on this six-month contract.

Some cities just feel good to be in. I returned many times to Barcelona since those initiations my first summer. Pete and I would always make plans to explore something new, inevitably ending up in the Gothic section for tapas and just watching the magnificent Spanish world go by.

Chapter 73:

THANKS FOR NOTHIN'

Somebody's very pink lipstick has left a permanent-looking tattoo on the well-worn Blarney Stone. I have to kiss THAT…?

After graduating from nursing school, my mother took a three-month trip throughout Europe. Her stories are the stuff of family legend, her photo album my first exposure to all the places that I dreamt of visiting. Her kissing of the Blarney Stone was photographed and when I found out that my ship would be going to Ireland, I figured that it would be perfect to replicate the picture with me kissing it thirty-five years later.

I escorted the tour to Blarney, enjoying the lush grounds of the castle with its surprisingly exotic flora. A younger group of passengers accompanied me and we sat in the warm wool factory to sip the complimentary Irish coffee included with our tour. (Don't mix the cream in on top. Sip the coffee through it! Who knew?)

Arriving at the actual castle, we hiked up past the old kitchen and dungeon to wait in line. I briefed a guy in my group on the workings of my camera and he agreed to take my "historical" photo as I kissed the famous stone.

The flexibility of previous fellow kissers who have to lie down and tilt their heads way back in order to kiss this thing is impressive. It's my turn. My glasses and hat are safely stowed away. I lean back and discover the lipstick. Grossed out and hurried, I have faith that my guy is taking the photo. I just PRETEND to give the cold rock a smack and quickly resume standing position, anticipating a view of my faux kiss on my digital camera. But instead, my guy just looks at me dumbly and says, 'Oh, I was watching you! I forgot to take your picture." And he just laughs it off!

Hello!

There is no turning back now! A huge line prevents recreating my passionate encounter with granite. Here I had done this whole climb, waited in line, given this inept man his "training", and even planted my kisser CLOSE to somebody's crusty coral pink lipstick only to find he has "forgotten"?

Yes, there are worse things. I could've paid the 12 euros ($15) the Castle People charged for their PROFESSIONAL photo, but not only was that a complete waste of money, they SENT it to you LATER!

Yeah, right. They're not going to get me on that one.

Chapter 74:

MY FAVORITE PORT EVER

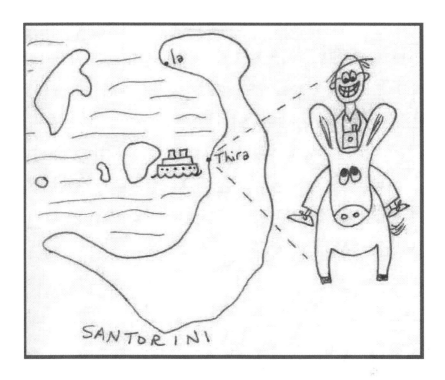

I am often asked what my favorite port is. Easily and without a doubt, my answer is Santorini, Greece. I would go back to vacation there in half a heartbeat!

Once a large volcanic island, Santorini literally exploded one day. Many scientists believe that this explosion doomed the lost city of Atlantis. A steep c-shaped bit of land, ships anchor where the middle of the island used to be within the huge caldera that now exists. The natural setting of Santorini strikes the senses even before debarking.

Once tendered to the land, the town of Thira is reached either by taking a cable car up, or riding a belled donkey for hundreds of steps that have been carved into the mountainside. Nose plugs and a strong sense of adventure come in handy with the latter option.

Suzannah and I escorted the Angelou Winery tour. Our jaws had to be scraped off of the tender deck before we could make our landings. We counted all of our passengers, loaded onto our busses, and wound our way up the treacherous road leading to the winery and its vineyards. What anticipation! That any life can be produced from such black and hopeless-looking landscape is a miracle.

Taken down into the roomy wine cellar, one window consisting of brown bottles stacked on their sides, the sun shone welcomingly through the glass. The tasting began. You just can't go wrong when alcohol is served on a tour. Any complaints brewing are usually forgotten while still in their germinal stages.

The winery overlooked the incredible blue of the sea and the other tiny islands that make up Santorini. The outdoor patio we stood on was constructed with stone, but the sidewalls and mortar in between the stone glistened pure white, creating an immaculate effect. Suzannah and I gulped ripe tomatoes soaked in perfect olive oil, fresh goat cheese, and my favorite, dolmades: stuffed grape leaves. Green olives were served, as well. We took lots of photos and had to remember, that although tipsy by eleven in the morning, we had escorting duties to attend to!

Everybody was happy.

EVERYBODY.

The scenery, the food, the wine, the friends, and the gorgeous, attentive servers at this establishment—nothing lacked.

Our trip continued to the town of Oia (pronounced EE-uh). It hangs off of the edge of the island as you near Santorini, white snow drifted on a brown cliff. Walking through the town was an Escher print come to life, an elaborate jungle gym. Just as one walkway leveled, I'd meet a turn, a staircase, or somebody's unexpected back yard with a pristine swimming pool daring to hang over a cliff edge. Arches with bells rose triumphantly over the stitched together landscape of buildings, creating a thrilling contrast with the shining Aegean down below.

Everything was painted white and looked new. The funniest thing to discover was that the blue church domes that all calendars and books label as "Greece" should really be labeled "Oia"! The tiny town represents the whole country for those who have never visited.

Endless exploring can be done. I found myself at the base of a functioning windmill where actual canvas sails propelled the ever-turning twelve arms. The structure's roof was straw, blowing in the breeze along with every white umbrella in town. Inns and restaurants hid away in little niches, fun to find, and all complete with their own marvelous sea views.

I bought some inexpensive and delicious pistachio nuts here and smiled to hear my guide say that the Grecian olive produces the best olive oil in the world. The various guides that I had in Italy, Spain, and Turkey said the same thing about their own country's olives, too.

I had always wanted to visit Greece and this island was what I imagined when I thought of the country—buildings of bold colors, tasty food, and unparalleled scenery. Ample shopping opportunities presented themselves in town, scooters could be rented to travel the island, and the archeological site at Acrotiri was open for exploration, activities that I'd have to experience later.

Sailing out of Santorini's caldera for the last time, a light breeze soothed my tired face. The stairway zigzagging its way up to Thira faded out. The windmill in Oia lazily rotated, and the blood red sun disappeared yet again into the Grecian haze.

Chapter 75:

AFTERWORD

Holland America's ss Rotterdam was sold to Premiere Cruises and became the Rembradt. Premiere went under and the Rott is now a floating hotel in the actual city of Rotterdam in the Netherlands.

I ported in Forteleza, Brazil with the Rembradt when I worked on the Royal Viking Sun, which in turn became Holland America's Prisendam.

The cruise ship industry is very reduce, reuse , recycle.

I ported in Amsterdam with the Prinsendam when I worked on the Cunard Caronia (formerly the Vistafjord), which became the Saga Ruby and is now a floating hotel under the name of Oasia.

It is wonderful to think that all the ships I worked on for three years are still out there providing happy memories for many other travelers of this great wide world.

I will treasure forever the memories that I have from all three of my cruise ships. Besides the amazing travel opportunities and lessons in the school of life, I value very much the lifelong friendships that I made while sailing. In such cramped spaces, relationships develop quickly and intensely! In fact, I know of two couples who met while under contract with me, who have since married and started families together.

But I think what I miss most are my times out on deck. There was nothing better than to go up for some very necessary fresh air and enjoy the relaxing sound of the waves as we cruised on to our next port of call. Late in the afternoon, the heat of the day would be dissipating. The passengers would be getting ready for their dinners and I usually felt as if I had the deck all to myself, engrossed in a wonderful book or a challenging crossword puzzle.

Best of all were the numerous and glorious sunsets, the open ocean serving as the ideal foreground. The water sparkles brilliantly. I am enthralled with the dancing reflections and constantly reminded to be grateful for my fantastic life at sea.

THE END

ACKNOWLEDGMENTS:

Endless thanks to Manya, Barb, Mom, Joe, and Amanda for listening to or reading early manuscripts of this book. Special thanks to Jenny for suggesting that I add the maps!

I also want to thank everyone who I ever worked with on ships. Obviously, there are too many to separately cite but I must list those that worked in the Shore Excursion offices and gave me all of the wonderful tours to escort: Nicola, Patrick, Lee, Sharon, Tosh, and Naomi, among several others. My cruise directors over those years deserve special mention, too, as they always provided enthusiastic support for me and my casts: Brian, Rick, Bob, Scott, Andrew, Martyn, and David. The cruise staff folks were always amazing, too. Special shout outs to Anja, Tanya (LASAGNA!!), Yvonne, and Julie.

And of course, none of my fabulous experiences asea would've been possible without my two producers Anita Mann and Morag Veljkovic.

Made in the USA
Middletown, DE
04 February 2017